Justification, Sanctification, *and* Union with Christ

Justification, Sanctification, *and* Union with Christ

Fresh Insights from Calvin, Westminster, and Walter Marshall

SHERIF A. FAHIM

Foreword by Joel R. Beeke

WIPF *&* STOCK · Eugene, Oregon

JUSTIFICATION, SANCTIFICATION, AND UNION WITH CHRIST
Fresh Insights from Calvin, Westminster, and Walter Marshall

Copyright © 2022 Sherif A. Fahim. All rights reserved. Except for brief quotations in critical publications or reviews, no part of this book may be reproduced in any manner without prior written permission from the publisher. Write: Permissions, Wipf and Stock Publishers, 199 W. 8th Ave., Suite 3, Eugene, OR 97401.

Wipf & Stock
An Imprint of Wipf and Stock Publishers
199 W. 8th Ave., Suite 3
Eugene, OR 97401

www.wipfandstock.com

PAPERBACK ISBN: 978-1-6667-3407-2
HARDCOVER ISBN: 978-1-6667-2954-2
EBOOK ISBN: 978-1-6667-2955-9

VERSION NUMBER 011322

Scripture quotations taken from the (NASB®) New American Standard Bible®, Copyright © 1995 by The Lockman Foundation. Used by permission. All rights reserved. www.lockman.org

And in all the land there were no women
so beautiful as Job's daughters. (Job 42:15)

To the most three beautiful daughters, Sophia, Nelly, and Naomi

Contents

Foreword by Joel R. Beeke | ix
Acknowledgments | xi
Introduction | xiii

CHAPTER 1
Calvin on the Relation between Justification and Sanctification | 1

CHAPTER 2
The Westminster Standards: The Relation between Justification and Sanctification | 22

CHAPTER 3
Marshall on Justification | 42

CHAPTER 4
Marshall on Sanctification | 62

CHAPTER 5
Walter Marshall: Power of the Gospel and Spiritual Growth | 91

Conclusion and Prospect | 115

Bibliography | 123

Foreword

The relationship between justification and sanctification is a point of controversy among theologians, especially Reformation and Roman Catholic theologians. However, it is also a point of concern for many people in their Christian lives as they struggle against doubts and fears while seeking assurance of salvation. Walter Marshall discovered this by personal experience.

A mid-seventeenth-century English Puritan divine, Marshall was ministering the gospel to others when he found himself in profound spiritual darkness and distress concerning his spiritual state. He was further confused by the swirling clouds of Neonomianism (turning the gospel into a new law fulfilled by faith) and antinomianism (against the law; i.e., Christians do not need to obey the moral law), stirred up by some of his fellow nonconformists in England. The light dawned after a conversation with Thomas Goodwin, and out of this insight and further meditation grew the book, *The Gospel Mystery of Sanctification*.

The great motif of *Gospel Mystery* is that sanctification, though a branch of salvation distinct from justification, grows out of the same root: union with Christ by a Spirit-worked faith in the gospel. Holiness is utterly foreign to people while they remain in the state of sin, and their efforts to attain it apart from Christ are misguided and doomed to failure. Good fruit will grow only after they are grafted into the root of the incarnate Lord. Having received Christ and continuing to rest upon him day by day, believers find the grace to walk with God in obedience to his commandments. The problem that Marshall faced, like many others, was placing the cart before the horse. The treatise *Gospel Mystery*, together with the sermon often published with it on justification, remind us that putting things in the right order can make all the difference.

Foreword

Given the importance of Marshall's book, it is with great pleasure that I commend to you Sherif Fahim's study of Marshall in the context of Calvin and the Westminster Assembly. Sherif, whom I have been privileged to know by his ThM and PhD studies at Puritan Reformed Theological Seminary, is a highly articulate scholar with a remarkably probing intellect. He does an excellent job of situating Marshall's teachings in the Reformed orthodoxy of the seventeenth century. Yet Sherif approaches theology not with the arid detachment of an academic isolated from real life, but with a pastor's heart that pulses with desire for people to abide in Christ's word, know the truth, and experience his liberating power (John 8:31–32). This makes Sherif even more qualified to teach us about the Puritans, who were driven by the same holy ambition.

May God use this study to clarify the relation of justification and sanctification in the theological system of early English Reformed theology, and to give many people the same experience of assurance and empowerment for holiness that Marshall himself experienced by faith in Jesus Christ.

—Joel R. Beeke

Acknowledgments

For this work to be accomplished, our gracious God used many people to help me in my journey to finish this manuscript. First of all, I would like to express my deep gratitude to my wife, Marian, and my three little daughters, Sophia, Nelly, and Naomi. In the midst of the hard work, they have always been a source of support and joy.

When I arrived at Puritan Reformed Theological Seminary to do my ThM in systematic theology, I wanted my thesis to be about the relationship between justification and sanctification. I owe an immense debt to my advisor Dr. Joel Beeke, the president of PRTS, whom I approached first regarding his advice about which of the Puritans has written on this topic. Although there is a plethora of resources, he, without hesitation, picked *The Gospel Mystery of Sanctification* and told me, "This is your book!" Dr. Beeke skillfully guided me to accomplish this work.

I offer my sincere thanks to Dr. Adriaan Neele, who helped me refine my research and improve my approach to historical theology. I am also deeply grateful to Mr. Karl Kwekel, who has been helping me in each step of this work, editing my English. I also wish to express my appreciation to the PRTS librarians, Laura Ladwig and Kim Dykema, who kept a constant stream of research materials flowing. Laura has been of great assistance to me in refining my footnotes and bibliography. A special thanks to my mentor, Frank Newell; through his unfailing prayers and encouragement, I was able to persevere.

Finally, my inexpressible gratitude is to my Lord Jesus Christ who led me through this work to deeper appreciation of his uniqueness. I am glad that in the five hundredth anniversary of the Reformation, I finished this project that emphasizes the unique centrality of Christ and his work in our justification and sanctification. To him be all glory and praise.

Solo Christo

Introduction

Various scholars have addressed several aspects of Walter Marshall's (1628–80) understanding of the doctrine of justification, the doctrine of sanctification, and the doctrine of the union with Christ. There is, however, a lack of attention on Marshall's understanding of the relationship between justification and sanctification, with the doctrine of union with Christ in view. This study will focus on that gap by examining Marshall's book *The Gospel Mystery of Sanctification* (1692), and his sermon on the doctrine of justification: "The Doctrine of Justification Explained and Applied." The historical theological context, in which Marshall's book was written will be considered, especially the concerns of legalism and Antinomianism.

In addressing these issues, Marshall's view will be prefaced by John Calvin's (1509–64) view about the relation between justification and sanctification; as well as the Westminster Assembly's (1643–53) teachings upon the same subjects. Subsequently, Marshall's views will be assessed in terms of continuity and discontinuity with Calvin and the Westminster Assembly.

This work will end with a conclusion including a practical application for the life of the church today.

Secondary Literature Review

Not much literature has been written on Walter Marshall's book. In the preface to the first edition of *The Gospel Mystery of Sanctification* the elusive N. N. gives a brief summary of Marshall's life and the way Marshall's book asserts the inseparable relation between holiness and happiness.[1] Another recommendatory preface was prefixed to the Edinburgh edition of 1733

---

1. N., "Preface".

which asserts that Marshall's work "leads the reader to Jesus Christ and gospel holiness against the Neonomian errors."[2] Adam Gib wrote another recommendation in the 1744 Edinburgh edition in which he argues that Marshall's book answers the errors of both Antinomianism and legalism.[3] Another one who expressed his great appreciation of Marshall's work is James Hervey. Hervey sent a letter to the publisher of the sixth edition of *The Gospel Mystery* in 1756, commending him for republishing the book. In a brief summary of Marshall's ideas, Herby writes "Mr. Marshall represents true holiness as consisting in the love of God and the love of man:—that unforced, unfeigned, and most rational love of God, which arises from a discovery of his unspeakable mercy and infinite kindness to us."[4]

Arthur Skevington Wood wrote a historical overview in 1958 about Walter Marshal, and *The Gospel Mystery of Sanctification*.[5] Another article about Walter Marshall is written by John Marshall and summarized Walter Marshall's fourteen directions and how his work addresses both Antinomianism and Neonomianism. However, the study lacked to address either union with Christ or the relation between justification and sanctification in Walter Marshall's theology.[6] Joel Beeke asserts, however, five lessons from *The Gospel Mystery of Sanctification*, (1) union with Christ and sanctification, (2) justification and sanctification, (3) Christ and his word, (4) the mind and soul, and (5) the sacred and the secular.[7] Although Beeke referred rightly to the importance of union with Christ and justification in relation to sanctification, he did not elaborate extensively about Marshall's view of these relations. Richard Ngun's work on the role of the law in sanctification among select Calvinists, includes Calvin, Martin Bucer (1491–1551), Ulrich Zwingli (1484–1531), John Hooper (1495–1555), Johannes Wollebius (1589–1629), William Ames (1576–1633), and the Westminster Confessions, but not Walter Marshall.[8] In his 2005 MDiv thesis, Bert Pohl only gave a very brief summary of Marshall's fourteen directions

---

2. Erskine et al., "Recommendatory Preface," vi.
3. Gib, "Recommendation by the Reverend Mr Adam Gib," vii.
4. Hervey, "Recommendation Letter," 328–29.
5. Wood, "Walter Marshall," 18–29.
6. Marshall, "Walter Marshall," 17–40.
7. Beeke, "Introduction".
8. Ngun, "Survey of the Role of the Law," 45–71.

without expanding on the way that justification and sanctification related in Marshall's view.⁹

The first doctoral dissertation written on Walter Marshall's theology argued that a discontinuity between Marshall and Keswick existed especially in relation to union with Christ,¹⁰ while another recent work on Marshall's theology is more concerned with Marshall's doctrine of sanctification in union with Christ in the context of the seventeenth-century Antinomian/Neonomian controversy.¹¹

Thus, some themes and aspects of Walter Marshall's work have been addressed, including Marshall's struggle against Antinomianism on the one side and Neonomianism on the other side, especially in relation to Baxter's work, and the union with Christ and its relation to sanctification in Marshall's view. However, less attention has been given in the area of Marshall's understanding of the relation between justification and sanctification, with the doctrine of union with Christ in view. This study seeks to fill this gap.

A proper assessment of Marshall's view on the relation between justification and sanctification is strengthened by discerning continuity and discontinuity of Marshall's thought in relation with Calvin and the Westminster Assembly. Calvin's ideas and writings were of great importance in the sixteenth and seventeenth century. This importance is emphasized by the number of English translations of Calvin's works in the sixteenth century, prior to and probably known by Marshall—the *Institutes of Christian Religion*,¹² and many of his commentaries and sermons, for example. In particular, the *Institutes*,¹³ sermons on Galatians and on Ephesians, and commentaries on Romans, Corinthians, and Galatians are indispensable for a study on justification, sanctification, and union with Christ. Furthermore, as Marshall's early life coincide with the era of the Westminster Assembly, this study will include an examination of the Assembly's confessional statements on the doctrines of justification, sanctification, and union with Christ.

---

9. Pohl, "Study of How the Gospel Is Effective."
10. Lee, "Sanctification by Faith."
11. Christ, "New Creation in Christ."
12. Calvin, *Inst.*
13. Calvin, *Inst.* 3.6–19.

Introduction

Statement of the Question: A Historical Theological Context

Walter Marshall was born in 1628 at Bishops Wearmouth in Durham, England and educated, becoming a fellow from 1648 to 1657 at New College in Oxford. Marshall served as a fellow of the College at Winchester till the Act of Uniformity in 1662 when he refused to conform to the Book of Common Prayer. As a result, he was ejected from the Church of England on Bartholomew's Day but was called to be pastor at an independent congregation at Gosport, Hampshire where he served for eighteen years until he died.

During this time, Marshall experienced troubled thoughts because of a sense of guilt. He tried many methods of mortification to experience peace of conscience with no success. Consequently, he consulted Richard Baxter (1615–91) whose writings Marshall was familiar with, but again without relief. Then in a life-changing consultation with the Westminster Divine, Thomas Goodwin (1600–1680), Marshall was convinced that the worst of his sins was the sin of unbelief in not believing in Christ for the remission of his sins and the sanctifying of his nature. Marshall was shown that the power of holiness is found in Christ and not in himself. Subsequently, he wrote *The Gospel Mystery of Sanctification*, gleaning the title from Paul's statement in 1 Tim 3:16, "Great is the mystery of godliness." The main theme of Marshall's work was that growing in holiness can only occur by the power of the gospel, and not by one's own strength. Marshall argued,

> This is a great mystery (contrary to the apprehensions, not only of the vulgar, but of some learned divines) that we must be reconciled to God and justified by the remission of our sins and imputation of righteousness, before any sincere obedience to the law.[14]

This sanctification or growth in holiness that is motivated by the power of the gospel is only real in light of our union with Christ. For Marshall, union with Christ

> is a privilege bestowed on believers in their very first entrance into a holy state, on which all ability to do good works depends, and all sincere obedience to the law follows after it, as fruit produced by it.[15]

---

14. Marshall, *Gospel Mystery of Sanctification*, 22.
15. Marshall, *Gospel Mystery of Sanctification*, 47.

Introduction

Hence, for Marshall the relationship of the doctrine of justification and sanctification can only be understood within the framework of one's understanding of the union with Christ.

Statement of the Question: A Justification of the Study

The historical theological context of *The Gospel Mystery of Sanctification*, then, shows the importance of Marshall's work on sanctification and on its relation to justification. Marshall's contribution is important in discussing how the two graces of justification and sanctification relate. He dug deeply, not only about growth in holiness but also about how the doctrine of justification and the message of the gospel are the basis for sanctification. The lack of attention in secondary scholarly literature on Marshall's articulation of the doctrines of justification, sanctification, and union with Christ, and their relationship to each other, highlights the need for this study to make a scholarly contribution in this area. Moreover, the quest for spiritual growth is highly relevant for believers in all times. Marshall's work may well be vitally important to help it grasp that the power of the gospel is the means to godliness. In this regard, the study seeks to contribute to the church today.

Research Method and Approach

This study falls under the heading of descriptive, analytical, historical theological research. In order to achieve the aim of this work, a careful study will be made of Calvin's view about the relation between justification and sanctification (chapter 1). This will include a review of his *Institutes*, New Testament commentaries and sermons, and engage with secondary literature.

The exposition of the relation between justification and sanctification as found in the Westminster Standards will be discussed in chapter 2. This discussion will include minutes of the Westminster Assembly, writings of the Westminster divines, such as Samuel Rutherford (1600–1661)[16] and Anthony Burgess (d. 1664),[17] and engage with secondary literature on the Westminster Assembly.

---

16. Ngun, "Survey of the Role of the Law," 45–71.
17. Burgess, *True Doctrine of Justification*.

Introduction

The core of the book will focus on Walter Marshall's work, and open with an assessment of Marshall's formulation of the doctrine of sin. Subsequently, attention will be given to Marshall's understanding of justification (chapter 3) and sanctification (chapter 4). Finally, a chapter will discuss the way Marshall understood the relation between justification and sanctification in light of union with Christ (chapter 5). These chapters will rest on primary source research, which includes *The Gospel Mystery of Sanctification*, and Marshall's sermon on justification entitled "The Doctrine of Justification Explained and Applied." Each chapter, though, will engage with relevant secondary literature. The final chapter, "Conclusion and Prospect," will contain concluding observations regarding the research and shows possible ways that Marshall's work is relevant for the church's preaching of the gospel today.

CHAPTER 1

Calvin on the Relation between Justification and Sanctification

Walter Marshall did not write his theology without any prior influence. As a reformed pastor, he must have been exposed to previous writings from other theologians. Calvin's ideas and writings were of great importance in the sixteenth and seventeenth century. This importance is emphasized by the number of English translations of Calvin's works in the sixteenth century, prior to and probably known by Marshall—the *Institutes of Christian Religion*,[1] and many of his commentaries and sermons, for example. In particular, the *Institutes*,[2] sermons on Galatians and on Ephesians, and commentaries on Romans, Corinthians, and Galatians are indispensable for a study on justification, sanctification, and union with Christ.

Joel Beeke rightly argues that "one of the famous charges against Calvinism is that it is an ivory tower school of thought, dealing in high and lofty doctrines that have no practical benefits for ordinary people in the church or society at large."[3] This charge is totally against what the Reformed theology really teaches. In fact, Calvin's writings show that what we believe and how we live are inseparable. Sinclair Ferguson argues that "when Calvin first published the *Institutes of the Christian Religion*, it bore the significant subtitle: *Containing the whole sum of piety* which shows that Calvin's

---

1. Calvin, *Inst.*
2. Calvin, *Inst.* 3.6–19.
3. Beeke, *Living For God's Glory*, 189.

purpose was not only intellectual but also spiritual."[4] Calvin was not just a theologian, but primarily he was a pastor so he was so keen to show how the doctrines that he was teaching and writing relate to our Christian life.

"Sanctification is the work of God's free grace, whereby we are renewed in the whole man after the image of God, and are enabled more and more to die unto sin, and live unto righteousness." This quotation is the answer of the *Westminster Shorter Catechism* for question 35, "What is Sanctification?" About 100 years earlier, Calvin believed that "sanctification is the result of God's grace irresistibly effected by the work of the Holy Spirit."[5] Considering Calvin's doctrine of sanctification may include what sanctification is; how sanctification relates to the twin grace that accompanies it, which is justification; and moreover, the foundation from which sanctification springs, that is union with Christ. The aim of this chapter is to investigate Calvin's view of sanctification and how it relates to justification. Discussing the relation between sanctification and justification will touch upon the meaning of sanctification and how it flows from union with Christ.

Sanctification and Union with Christ

William Edgar argues that "the structure of Calvin's institutes can be understood generally as moving from themes that relate to the first, the second, and the third persons of the Godhead."[6] So in book 1, Calvin begins with the Father: "The Knowledge of God the Creator." Then as Randall Gleason argues, "in book three of the *Institutes*, Calvin explains how the believer receives by the work of the Holy Spirit the gracious benefits of the mediatorial work of Christ (the Son) described in book two."[7] This idea is expressed in the title which Calvin gave to book 3 in his *Institutes*:[8] "The Way in Which We Receive the Grace of Christ: What Benefits Come to Us from It, and What Effects Follow."[9]

    4. Ferguson, "Reformed View," 48.
    5. Partee, *Theology of John Calvin*, 208.
    6. Edgar, "Ethics," 320.
    7. Gleason, *John Calvin and John Owen*, 53.
    8. In book 4 Calvin continues to explain the work of the Holy Spirit under the title "The External Means or Aims by Which God Invites Us into the Society of Christ and Holds Us Therein."
    9. Calvin, *Inst.* 3.1.1.

The first work of the Spirit that Calvin began with in book three is the union with Christ. According to Bert Pohl, Calvin teaches that "the Holy Spirit plays an active role in initiating and maintaining this union."[10] In fact, "the Holy Spirit is the bond of this union."[11] Calvin believes that "by the power of his (Christ's) Spirit, he makes us a part of his body, so that from him we derive our life."[12] Calvin also commented about the sacred union between Jesus and the believers saying that "the Son conveyed Himself entirely into us by the efficacy of His Spirit."[13]

Also, Calvin says that faith unites us to Christ. For Calvin, "faith does not reconcile us to God at all unless it joins us to Christ."[14] William Wright argues that "many interpreters of Calvin believe that Calvin's use of faith in the beginning of book three was to make the transition from 'objective' to 'subjective,' from Christ's work to our own union with Christ."[15] But this faith is also "the principal work of the Holy Spirit."[16] We cannot generate faith on our own because of our natural inability that "man's mind can become spiritually wise only in so far as God illumines it."[17] Therefore, for Calvin, "our union with Christ, being fundamental to our sanctification, has two bonds: from God's perspective it is the Holy Spirit and from man's perspective it is our faith."[18] However, as Gleason argues, "by affirming that faith is a gift from God, Calvin maintains God's gracious initiative in uniting us to Christ."[19]

Calvin expressed how central this union with Christ to his theology when he says "First, we must understand that as long as Christ remains outside of us, and we are separated from him, all that he has suffered and done for the salvation of the human race remains useless and of no value for us."[20] By the power of the Spirit, "Christ imparts to us His life and all the

---

10. Pohl, "Study of How the Gospel Is Effective," 11.
11. Gleason, *John Calvin and John Owen*, 54.
12. Calvin, *Calvin's Commentaries*, Eph 5:31.
13. Calvin, *Calvin's Commentaries*, John 14:20.
14. Calvin, *Inst.* 3.2.30.
15. Wright, *Calvin's Salvation in Writing*, 189.
16. Calvin, *Inst.* 3.1.4.
17. Calvin, *Inst.* 2.2.20.
18. Pohl, "Study of How the Gospel Is Effective," 12.
19. Gleason, *John Calvin and John Owen*, 55.
20. Calvin, *Inst.* 3.1.1.

blessings which He has received from the Father."[21] Calvin's teaching opposes any notion of Antinomianism or moral carelessness that may result from the union with Christ.[22] Charles Partee argues that in Calvin's theology, "there is an inseparable bond among Jesus Christ, grace, faith, justification, and sanctification."[23] For Calvin, "no sanctification exists apart from communion with Christ,"[24] and "no communion can exist without love."[25] Therefore, "union with Christ results in the sanctification of the Spirit since the Holy Spirit mediates the sanctifying benefits of the cross."[26]

Union with Christ: Channel of Double Grace

Calvin believed that two blessings must result from union with Christ, which are justification and sanctification. He coined the term "double grace" to express the reality that sanctification as proceeding part and parcel with justification.[27] In his *Institutes* Calvin expressed this truth in the following words: "By partaking of him [Christ], we principally receive a double grace: namely, that being reconciled to God through Christ's blamelessness, we may have in heaven instead of a Judge a gracious Father; and secondly, that sanctified by Christ's spirit we may cultivate blamelessness and purity of life."[28]

The idea of the double grace was also clear in Calvin's commentaries. In his commentary on 1 Cor 1:30, Calvin writes:

> We cannot be justified freely through faith alone without at the same time living holily. For these fruits of grace are connected together, as it were, by an indissoluble tie, so that he who attempts to sever them does in a manner tear Christ in pieces. Let therefore the man who seeks to be justified through Christ, by God's unmerited goodness, consider that this cannot be attained without his taking him at the same time for sanctification.[29]

21. Calvin, *Calvin's Commentaries*, John 17:21.
22. Cameron, "How 'Ethics' Works," 242.
23. Partee, *Theology of John Calvin*, 209.
24. Calvin, *Inst.* 3.14.4.
25. Calvin, *Calvin's Commentaries*, 1 John 2:5.
26. Gleason, *John Calvin and John Owen*, 54–55.
27. Pohl, "Study of How the Gospel Is Effective," 8.
28. Calvin, *Inst.* 3.11.1.
29. Calvin, *Calvin's Commentaries*, 1 Cor 1:30.

Also, in Calvin's commentary on Gal 2:20, he says "Christ lives in us in two ways. The one life consists in governing us by his Spirit and directing all our actions [sanctification]; the other, in making us partakers of his righteousness; so that, while we can do nothing of ourselves, we are accepted in the sight of God [justification]."[30]

Therefore, Calvin is tying our union with Christ into both justification and sanctification. We can be righteous in the presence of God through both the remission of sin and imputation of righteousness only from Christ.[31] "Do you wish, then, to attain righteousness in Christ? You must first possess Christ; but you cannot possess Him without being made partaker in His sanctification."[32] Thomas Hawkes summarizes Calvin's view as he says, "this double grace as coming through the work of Christ, means that we can look to Christ for our continued progress in holiness."[33]

Sanctification and Justification

For Calvin the relation between justification and sanctification is "the basic principle of the whole doctrine of salvation, the foundation of all religion" (sermon on Luke 1:5–10; *Ionnais Calvini opera quae supersunt omnia* 46:23).[34] It is noteworthy that two sections in the *Institutes* deal with on the Christian life: chapters 6–10 and chapters 17–19 in book 3. "Sandwiched between these two sections is a full discussion of justification by faith (chapters 11–16)."[35]

The question here is why did his exposition on sanctification precede rather than follow the exposition on justification? As Partee writes, "the normal, logical, and historical progression is from justification to sanctification whereupon God first forgives our sins and only then mandates the holy life."[36] Calvin expressed this line of thought when he said, "Unless you first of all grasp what your relationship to God is, and the nature of his judgment concerning you, you have neither a foundation on which to

---

30. Calvin, *Calvin's Commentaries*, Gal 2:20.
31. Calvin, *Inst.* 3.11.2.
32. Calvin, *Inst.* 3.16.1.
33. Hawkes, "Pious Pastors," 34.
34. Partee, *Theology of John Calvin*, 209.
35. Edgar, "Ethics," 321.
36. Partee, *Theology of John Calvin*, 210.

establish your salvation nor one on which to build piety toward God."[37] If Calvin held this kind of progression, then why did he place justification in the middle of a larger discussion on sanctification?

This question has more than a single answer. William Edgar suggests that "Calvin wanted to head off possible objections from the Roman Catholics who would accuse him of Antinomianism (*libertinage*)."[38] The Roman Catholics believed that the Protestant view of justification by faith alone leads to a denial of the fruits of the Spirit and the holy life. As Hawkes says, "Calvin had in mind defending the reality that good works flow from, rather than are hindered by, free justification."[39]

Partee suggests another reason for such an arrangement, which is "Calvin's concern that Protestants might accept the activity of God in justification with such eagerness as to become inattentive to their own responsibility in sanctification."[40] Timothy Gwin writes, "Calvin, as a man of his times, made a conscious decision to describe the core of the Christian life by the term *pietas*."[41] As Edgar comments, "he was so concerned for piety and true sanctification that he sees justification here as a means as much as an end."[42] According to Calvin, "the whole life of Christians ought to be a sort of practice of godliness, for we have been called to sanctification."[43] Calvin's arrangement of sanctification and justification in the *Institutes* showed that "he was developing a confession of faith rather than a system of philosophical theology."[44]

Finally, Calvin's arrangement of material in book 3 drives home the point that justification and sanctification are inseparable.[45] This final point leads us to the next part of the paper which will dig deeper into the relation between justification and sanctification in Calvin's view.

---

37. Calvin, *Inst.* 3.11.1.
38. Edgar, "Ethics," 321.
39. Hawkes, "Pious Pastors," 34.
40. Partee, *Theology of John Calvin*, 210.
41. Gwin, "Mind and Heart Aflame," 3.
42. Edgar, "Ethics," 321–22.
43. Calvin, *Inst.* 3.19.2.
44. Partee, *Theology of John Calvin*, 211.
45. Edgar, "Ethics," 322.

Different yet Inseparable

While the Roman Catholic theology tended to confuse justification and sanctification, Calvin was very clear in showing that justification and sanctification are not identical, yet they are inseparable. Partee argues that this accurate description of Calvin's view is important because "if justification is too strongly emphasized, Calvin is moved in a Lutheran direction; if sanctification is too strongly emphasized, Calvin is moved in a Wesleyan direction."[46] Both justification and sanctification are inseparable so it is both improper and impossible to tear asunder the two concepts.[47] One of Calvin contemporaries who mixed justification and sanctification was Osiander.[48] Calvin refuted Osiander's views by showing that although distinct in meaning, justification and sanctification can never be separated in the Christian's life. "Christ cannot be torn into parts, so these two which we perceive in Him together and conjointly are inseparable—namely, righteousness and sanctification."[49]

"Justification and sanctification are one in divine origin and one in human experience."[50] Calvin expressed their inseparability saying, "But, since the question concerns only righteousness and sanctification, let us dwell upon these. Although we may distinguish them, Christ contains both of them inseparably in himself."[51]

However while bestowed concurrently, "the twin benefits are given in such a way that sanctification is still truly distinct from justification."[52] According to Partee, "Calvin saw justification as a completed fact which is accomplished *for* us while he saw sanctification as a continuing process which is accomplished *with* us."[53] Calvin believed that Paul teaches in Romans 8 that "condemnation which we of ourselves deserve has been swallowed up by the salvation that is in Christ."[54] The language of condemnation has to do with justification, so when Calvin said that our condemnation has

---

46. Partee, *Theology of John Calvin*, 209.
47. Hawkes, "Pious Pastors," 34.
48. Calvin, *Inst.* 3.11.6.
49. Calvin, *Inst.* 3.11.6.
50. Partee, *Theology of John Calvin*, 211.
51. Calvin, *Inst.* 3.16.1.
52. Garcia, *Life in Christ*, 77.
53. Partee, *Theology of John Calvin*, 211.
54. Calvin, *Inst.* 3.2.24.

been swallowed, he believed that our justification is accomplished. On the other hand, Calvin emphasized the reality that sanctification is a process as he said, "Not only does he [Christ] cleave to us by an indivisible bond of fellowship, but with a wonderful communion, day by day, he grows more and more into one body with us, until he becomes completely one with us."[55] In Calvin's commentary on the gospel of John, he said, "we ought to infer from Christ's words, that *sanctification* is not instantly completed in us on the first day, but that we make progress in it through the whole course of our life."[56] According to Calvin, although justification and sanctification are strongly connected to each other, they should never be confused. This tension is well expressed in Calvin's refutation of Osiander's teaching in the *Institutes*:

> For since God, for the preservation of righteousness, renews those whom he freely reckons as righteous, Osiander mixes that gift of regeneration with this free acceptance and contends that they are one and the same. Yet Scripture, even though it joins them, still lists them separately in order that God's manifold grace may better appear to us.[57]

In describing the proper relationship between justification and sanctification, Antinomianism and Roman Catholicism were not the only dangers that Calvin was facing. The other danger that Calvin also opposed was the perfectionism adopted by some Anabaptists. Partee writes, "Calvin objected that certain Anabaptists thought that they have been restored to perfect holiness and in following the Spirit no longer need to bridle the lusts of the flesh."[58] Gregg Allison asserts that "while desiring that all believers eagerly pursue and attain this inward conformity to Christ, Calvin was a realist."[59] Calvin knew that "he could not strictly demand evangelical perfection that he would not acknowledge as a Christian one who has not yet attained it."[60]

The Anabaptists' belief in perfection made them say that the sinner who has lapsed after he has received grace has no hope of pardon.[61] Calvin

55. Calvin, *Inst.* 3.2.24.
56. Calvin, *Calvin's Commentaries*, John 17:17.
57. Calvin, *Inst.* 3.11.6.
58. Partee, *Theology of John Calvin*, 210.
59. Allison, *Historical Theology*, 533.
60. Calvin, *Inst.* 3.6.5.
61. Calvin, *Inst.* 4.1.23.

objected any notion of perfectionism in this life. For Calvin, "the Lord's command to the saints in the Lord's prayer that says "Forgive us our debts" (Matt 6:12) repeatedly shows how imperfect they are; and their petition is not in vain because God promised to grant them forgiveness."[62] In Calvin's commentary on Eph 1:4 he also opposes perfectionism and says "The inference, too, which the Catharists, Celestines, and Donatists drew from these words, that we may attain perfection in this life, is without foundation. This is the goal to which the whole course of our life must be directed, and we shall not reach it till we have finished our course."[63] Also Calvin's teaching about continuous mortification of the flesh and vivification of the spirit as component parts of repentance in the life of saints shows that repentance is a lifelong process.[64]

So according to Calvin, when we believe, "we are regenerated and we are restored by this regeneration through the benefit of Christ into the righteousness of God; from which we had fallen through Adam."[65] However, Calvin also asserted that believers are still sinners whom although freed through regeneration from bondage to sin, yet in whom there remains a smoldering cinder of evil that can burst forth in flame at any time.[66]

The following quotation summarize Calvin's view about gradual sanctification:

> This restoration does not take place in one moment or one day or one year; but through continual and sometimes even slow advances God wipes out in his elect the corruptions of the flesh, cleanses them of guilt, consecrates them to himself as temples renewing all their minds to true purity that they may practice repentance throughout their lives and know that this warfare will end only at death.[67]

Then for Calvin, the union with Christ is not only a state but a process.[68] We are freed from the dominion of sin when we are engrafted into Christ; not that we immediately cease entirely to sin, but that we become at

---

62. Calvin, *Inst.* 4.1.23.
63. Calvin, *Calvin's Commentaries*, Eph 1:4.
64. Calvin, *Inst.* 3.3.8.
65. Calvin, *Inst.* 3.3.9.
66. Calvin, *Inst.* 3.3.10.
67. Calvin, *Inst.* 3.3.9.
68. Partee, *Theology of John Calvin*, 209.

last victorious in the contest.[69] Calvin believed that "sin does not reign in the believer, but sin continues to dwell."[70]

Accordingly, while affirming the imperfection of our present Christian life, Calvin also asserted that the conformity to Christ's life "ought to be desired and that we must strive towards it."[71] His expression on the tension between the imperfections and the endeavors of the Christian life being quite practical and reasonable[72] is found in the following lines:

> Let us not despair at the slightness of our success; for even though attainment may not correspond to desire, when today outstrips yesterday the effort is not lost. Only let us look toward our mark with sincere simplicity and aspire to our goal; not fondly flattering ourselves, nor excusing our own evil deeds, but with continuous effort striving toward this end: that we may surpass ourselves in goodness until we attain to goodness itself.[73]

To conclude, "based on our union with Christ, Calvin's development of the process of sanctification affirms that we are not justified by works but also not without works."[74] For Calvin, justification and sanctification are inseparably joined together, "just as the brightness of the sun cannot be separated from its heat. When we say that the sun is hot, it will most likely be shining at the same time, yet the brilliance of the sun is not the same as its heat."[75] This inseparable relation between the two distinct blessings of justification and sanctification is emphasized by many ways in Calvin's writings.

First: Man's Two Problems

First of all, for Calvin, justification and sanctification achieve the twofold cleansing needed to restore what happened to human beings in the fall. We sons of Adam have two main problems because of the fall: the imputed guilt and moral corruption. Our main problems are not only the actual sins that

---

69. Calvin, *Calvin's Commentaries*, Rom 6:6.
70. Partee, *Theology of John Calvin*, 210.
71. Calvin, *Inst.* 3.6.5.
72. Allison, *Historical Theology*, 533.
73. Calvin, *Inst.* 3.6.5.
74. Partee, *Theology of John Calvin*, 215.
75. Calvin, *Sermons on Galatians*, 198–99.

we commit daily and make us guilty before God, but also what is known as "original sin" which includes both guilt and pollution.[76]

Calvin comments on Acts 15:9 saying:

> We must now see how the grace of Christ does make us clean, that we may please God. And there is a double manner of purging, because Christ does offer and present us clean and just in the sight of his Father, by putting away our sins daily, which he has once purged by his blood; secondly, because, by mortifying the lusts of the flesh by his Spirit, he reforms us unto holiness of life.[77]

We as sinners have two distinct problems—guilt and corruption—that are also connected to each other. Justification and sanctification, which are also distinct yet inseparable, solve these two problems together. Justification is more related to our guilt while sanctification is related to our pollution. It is noteworthy that after Adam's fall we became directly into a state of deserving condemnation (Rom 5:12), and in justification "Christ's salvation wipes out our condemnation; with his worthiness he intercedes that your unworthiness may not come before God's sight."[78] On the other side, "after Adam's fall into sin, the image of God in us was not annihilated but perverted,"[79] i.e., polluted.

Here are a few notable observations here. In the fall, we were separated immediately from God, we had the verdict of "guilty" and our nature was corrupted, however we did not lose completely the image of God. In restoration, when we believe in Christ our guilt is dealt with immediately, and we have the verdict of "justified" and we become at peace with God (justification). Yet the restoration to the image of God in us and ending the corruption is a process that continues till we die (sanctification) our remaining lives. The other observation is that in the fall, as a necessary implication of our involvement in Adam's guilt, all human beings are born into a state of corruption.[80] In salvation, we grasp our new relationship to God, being justified in his eyes; at that time, we have a foundation on which we establish our salvation and build piety toward God.[81]

---

76. Hoekema, *Created in God's Image*, 148.
77. Calvin, *Calvin's Commentaries*, Acts 15:9.
78. Calvin, *Inst.* 3.2.24.
79. Hoekema, *Created in God's Image*, 83.
80. Hoekema, *Created in God's Image*, 150.
81. Calvin, *Inst.* 3.11.1.

Second: The Gospel Invitation

Calvin emphasized the inseparability of justification and sanctification by showing that both are reflected in the two headings which constitute the whole gospel: repentance and forgiveness of sins.[82] The reformer saw that repentance and forgiveness of sins are interrelated, as the Evangelists say: "John came preaching a baptism of repentance for the remission of sins" (Mark 1:4; Luke 3:3).[83]

God intends that both forgiveness of sins and repentance are to be preached. For Calvin we preach forgiveness of sins through Christ, our redemption and righteousness, by whose name men are accounted righteous and innocent in God's sight (justification). We also preach repentance in the name of Christ so that men may know their corruption and their need to be reborn again (sanctification).[84] Calvin saw this strong connection while describing the gospel that Christ and the apostles preached

> Therefore, when he (Christ) meant to summarize the whole gospel in brief, he said that he "should suffer, . . . rise from the dead, and that repentance and forgiveness of sins should be preached in his name" (Luke 24:26, 46–47). And after his resurrection the apostles preached this: "God raised Jesus . . . to give repentance to Israel and forgiveness of sins" (Acts 5:30–31).[85]

We must note that Calvin interpreted repentance as regeneration, "whose sole end is to restore in us the image of God that had been disfigured and all but obliterated through Adam's transgression."[86] Edgar writes, "the general term that encompasses the Christian life for Calvin is 'regeneration' which is unlike our modern tendency to reduce regeneration to the moment of the new birth."[87] Therefore, Calvin saw repentance as a lifestyle for the believer through which the process of sanctification occurs.

Then, according to Calvin, justification and sanctification both equally and jointly constitute God's redemptive purpose for the believer, and this purpose is expressed by the two expressions: repentance and forgiveness

---

82. Calvin, *Inst.* 3.3.19.
83. Calvin, *Inst.* 3.3.19.
84. Calvin, *Inst.* 3.3.19.
85. Calvin, *Inst.* 3.3.19.
86. Calvin, *Inst.* 3.3.9.
87. Edgar, "Ethics," 322.

of sins.[88] The way Calvin saw forgiveness of sins as a reference to justification and repentance (regeneration) as a reference to sanctification is well illustrated in his commentary upon 1 Cor 1:30. While answering those who charged him of being antinomian because he taught justification by faith alone without any works, he answered them commenting on 1 Cor 1:30 and said, "Those, however, that slander us, as if by preaching a free justification through faith we called men off from good works, are amply refuted from this passage, which intimates that faith apprehends in Christ regeneration equally with forgiveness of sins."[89] Using the forgiveness of sins and repentance language shows how inseparable justification and sanctification are and even more shows how they should be carefully distinguished.

Third: God's Eternal Decree

Another way of showing that justification and sanctification are inseparable in Calvin's teachings is to point to their presence in God's eternal decree. Although believers are not subjectively justified nor sanctified until the Holy Spirit in due time actually applies Christ unto them, according to Calvin both are to be found in the eternal decree of God. In the *Institutes*, we find that Calvin while explaining the relation between God's election and his foreknowledge, argued that "predestination to grace is subordinate to election to life."[90] In other words, the grace of justification is predestined in God's eternal decree to those "whom the possession of glory has long since been assigned."[91]

For Calvin, not only is justification found in God's eternal decree but also sanctification. Calvin comments on Paul's words in Eph 1:4 and says that "all our holiness and purity of life flow from the election of God."[92] Furthermore, Calvin says that the foundation and first cause, both of our calling and of all the benefits which we receive from God is his eternal election.[93]

---

88. Gleason, *John Calvin and John Owen*, 57.
89. Calvin, *Calvin's Commentaries*, 1 Cor 1:30.
90. Calvin, *Inst.* 3.22.9.
91. Calvin, *Inst.* 3.22.9.
92. Calvin, *Calvin's Commentaries*, Eph 1:4.
93. Calvin, *Calvin's Commentaries*, Eph 1:4.

Against those who try to say that the doctrine of election promotes antinomian way of life, Calvin answers in a way that shows how election, justification, and sanctification are attached to each other. He says

> We learn also from these words, that election gives no occasion to licentiousness, or to the blasphemy of wicked men who say, "Let us live in any manner we please; for, if we have been elected, we cannot perish." Paul tells them plainly, that they have no right to separate holiness of life from the grace of election; for "whom he did predestinate, them he also called, and whom he called, them he also justified."[94]

Fourth: In Christ

Pohl comments on the inseparability of justification and sanctification in Calvin's teaching by saying that "they are joined in Christ and must also be joined in us."[95] According to Calvin these two blessings are inseparable as they find their common source in the redemptive work of Jesus Christ. As we note earlier, for Calvin union with Christ is very central to our Christian life because through this unity that we have this double grace: justification and sanctification. About justification and its relationship to the death of Christ Calvin says, "What is it that gives us the boldness to lift up our eyes to heaven and call him our Father? . . . It is the fact that our sins are no longer imputed to us, since we continually resort to the cleansing obtained for us by the sufferings and death of the Lord Jesus Christ."[96]

Regarding sanctification and how it is rooted in Christ and his work, Calvin comments on Rom 6:5 and says that being united to Christ does not only designate "a conformity of example, but a secret union, by which we are joined to him; so that he, reviving us by his Spirit, transfers his own virtue to us."[97] In other words, "Sanctification is neither self-induced nor created in us by divine fiat; rather it has to be "earthed" in our world, that is in Christ's work for us in history."[98]

---

94. Calvin, *Calvin's Commentaries*, Eph 1:4.
95. Pohl, "Study of How the Gospel Is Effective," 9.
96. Calvin, *Sermons on Galatians*, 198.
97. Calvin, *Calvin's Commentaries*, Rom 6:5.
98. Ferguson, "Reformed View," 50.

Calvin expressed how Christ and his work is the reservoir from which all our needs, including justification and sanctification are supplied in the following lines

> We see that our whole salvation and all its parts are comprehended in Christ [Acts 4:12]. We should therefore take care not to derive the least portion of it from anywhere else. If we seek salvation, we are taught by the very name of Jesus that it is "of him" [1 Cor. 1:30]. If we seek any other gifts of the Spirit, they will be found in his anointing. If we seek strength, it lies in his dominion; if purity, in his conception; if gentleness, it appears in his birth. For by his birth he was made like us in all respects [Heb. 2:17] that he might learn to feel our pain [cf. Heb. 5:2]. If we seek redemption, it lies in his passion; if acquittal, in his condemnation; if remission of the curse, in his cross [Gal. 3:13]; if satisfaction, in his sacrifice; if purification, in his blood; if reconciliation, in his descent into hell; if mortification of the flesh, in his tomb; if newness of life, in his resurrection; if immortality, in the same; if inheritance of the Heavenly Kingdom, in his entrance into heaven; if protection, if security, if abundant supply of all blessings, in his Kingdom; if untroubled expectation of judgment, in the power given to him to judge. In short, since rich store of every kind of good abounds in him, let us drink our fill from this fountain, and from no other.[99]

William Wright writes that according to Calvin, "we are in Christ both reconciled with God and are, in some true sense of "to be," righteous and obedient servants."[100] Calvin argued from 1 Cor 1:30 that Christ is our righteousness, and that "the apostle Paul does not say that He [Christ] was sent to help us attain righteousness but himself to be our righteousness (1 Cor 1:30)."[101] Therefore, the dynamic of sanctification and the whole life of the Christian is to be found in union with Christ.

Fifth: By Faith

According to Calvin, both justification and sanctification can only be attained by faith. He states clearly in the *Institutes*, "Now, both repentance and forgiveness of sins—that is, newness of life and free reconciliation—are

---

99. Calvin, *Inst.* 2.16.19.
100. Wright, *Calvin's Salvation in Writing*, 194.
101. Calvin, *Inst.* 3.15.5.

conferred on us by Christ, and both are attained by us through faith."[102] For Calvin, by means of faith we possess Christ as offered to us by the Father.[103] "Christ is not offered only for righteousness, forgiveness of sins, and peace, but is also offered for sanctification."[104] Calvin's view binds together justification and sanctification with faith.

We must note that Calvin denies any notion that faith is a kind of work that we present to God in order to be justified or sanctified. Calvin comments on the meaning of faith and says,

> Now *faith* brings nothing to God, but, on the contrary, places man before God as empty and poor, that he may be filled with Christ and with his grace. It is, therefore, if we may be allowed the expression, a passive work, to which no reward can be paid, and it bestows on man no other righteousness than that which he receives from Christ.[105]

Calvin believed that only through faith do we obtain free righteousness by the mercy of God.[106]

Calvin also saw the relation between faith and repentance, which is the newness of life as the latter flowing from the former. He says, "Now it ought to be a fact beyond controversy that repentance not only constantly follows faith, but is also born of faith."[107] Calvin argues in this way because he believed that we cannot repent without knowing the grace of God which we uphold by faith. He expressed this line of thought as follows: "We mean to show that a man cannot apply himself seriously to repentance without knowing himself to belong to God. But no one is truly persuaded that he belongs to God unless he has first recognized God's grace."[108] Therefore, for Calvin, "we are not united to God because of our holiness but because of our union to Him we become more and more holy."[109]

Randall Gleason gives a good conclusion about Calvin's view about justification and sanctification being inseparable in relation to faith. Gleason says, "Calvin affirms that faith not only results in a declared righteousness

---

102. Calvin, *Inst.* 3.3.1.
103. Calvin, *Calvin's Commentaries*, John 6:29.
104. Calvin, *Inst.* 3.2.8.
105. Calvin, *Calvin's Commentaries*, John 6:29.
106. Calvin, *Inst.* 3.11.1.
107. Calvin, *Inst.* 3.3.1.
108. Calvin, *Inst.* 3.3.2.
109. Partee, *Theology of John Calvin*, 210.

but necessarily produces a righteousness of character thus inseparably binding both justification and sanctification together in the experience of the believer."[110]

Sixth: God's Work

For Calvin, both justification and sanctification are God's work not only objectively in the work of Christ but also subjectively in our lives. Calvin's use of faith in book 3 of the *Institutes* could make us infer that salvation depends on something about us or something we do.[111] But this inference is contrary to what Calvin himself said in the *Institutes*, for he asserted that assurance of salvation can never be attained as long as we depend on anything in ourselves.[112] Wright argues that "to understand book 3 as presenting the anthropological correlate to the Christocentric presentation in book 2 would be a mistake, for book 3 remains theological, although focusing on the Holy Spirit working in us."[113]

Reading Calvin carefully shows that justification and sanctification are both God's work. Partee says, "Calvin teaches that our justification occurs outside us in Christ's work for us."[114] For Calvin, when we are justified, the efficient cause is the mercy of God, the meritorious is Christ, the instrumental is the word in connection with faith.[115] Therefore, for Calvin, our actual justification before God is God's work in which the believer grasps the righteousness of Christ through faith, "and being clothed in it, appears in God's sight not as a sinner but as a righteous man."[116]

Regarding sanctification, Calvin argues that it is the work of the Holy Spirit within us. He rejects the concept of cooperation which says that we cooperate with the assisting grace of God.[117] Calvin believes that Phil 2:13 does not say that our hearts are simply turned or stirred up, or that the infirmity of a good will is helped, but that "a good inclination is wholly the

---

110. Gleason, *John Calvin and John Owen*, 58.
111. Wright, *Calvin's Salvation in Writing*, 190.
112. Calvin, *Inst.* 3.19.2.
113. Wright, *Calvin's Salvation in Writing*, 190.
114. Partee, *Theology of John Calvin*, 211.
115. Calvin, *Calvin's Commentaries*, Rom 3:22.
116. Calvin, *Inst.* 3.11.2.
117. Calvin, *Inst.* 2.2.6.

work of God without any reservation."[118] Calvin's view about sanctification being the work of God is strongly explained in the following lines

> We know, however, that under the term *sanctification* is included the entire renovation of the man. The Thessalonians, it is true, had been in part renewed, but Paul desires that God would perfect what is remaining. From this we infer, that we must, during our whole life, make progress in the pursuit of holiness. But if it is the part of God to renew the whole man, there is nothing left for free will. For if it had been our part to co-operate with God, Paul would have spoken thus—"May God aid or promote your sanctification." But when he says, *sanctify you wholly*, he makes him the sole Author of the entire work.[119]

Although Calvin emphasized that sanctification is God's work in our lives, he did not deny the believer's active involvement in sanctification.[120] But Calvin, as we affirmed, did not see the believer's involvement as cooperation with God's grace that results in our sanctification. Rather, Calvin says, "We ourselves are fitly doing what God's Spirit is doing in us, even if our will contributes nothing of itself distinct from his grace."[121] In other words, Calvin is saying that by the work of the Holy Spirit in the believer, "God's action within human action is simultaneously that person's action."[122] Calvin expressed this view in his commentary on Rom 6:11 as he says,

> As Christ once died for the purpose of destroying sin, so you have once died, that in future you may cease from sin; yea, you must daily proceed with that work of mortifying, which is begun in you, till sin be wholly destroyed: as Christ is raised to an incorruptible life, so you are regenerated by the grace of God, that you may lead a life of holiness and righteousness, inasmuch as the power of the Holy Spirit, by which ye have been renewed, is eternal, and shall ever continue the same.[123]

Therefore, Calvin's view of sanctification as God's work in the life of the believer was not promoting Antinomianism. Calvin was not denying

---

118. Calvin, *Calvin's Commentaries*, Phil 2:13.
119. Calvin, *Calvin's Commentaries*, 1 Thess 5:23.
120. Gleason, *John Calvin and John Owen*, 58.
121. Calvin, *Inst.* 2.5.15.
122. Partee, *Theology of John Calvin*, 213.
123. Calvin, *Calvin's Commentaries*, Rom 6:11.

the involvement of the Christian. But he did not see the believer's involvement as his cooperative role in the process of sanctification. Rather, Calvin saw that God's grace in sanctification makes human participation possible. "This grace enables the Christian to struggle effectually against sin and progress towards conformity to Christ."[124] Therefore, Calvin says, "You act and are acted upon. And if you are acted upon by one who is good, then you act well."[125] Gleason writes "Calvin declares that God's sanctifying work is in the indicative mood which is demonstrated, in turn by the believer's active obedience in the imperatives."[126]

Justification: Spring of Sanctification

We have seen how Calvin maintains the inseparability of justification and sanctification. He saw these two blessings as a double grace that we enjoy in our union with Christ. For Calvin, justification and sanctification are not just two blessings that happen together in the life of the believer due to his union with Christ. A relationship exists between them in which one of them leads to the other. In contrast to the Roman Catholic theology, which believes that sanctification would lead to justification, Calvin believed that justification is the prerequisite from which sanctification necessarily follows. He comments on Rom 6:2 and says, "The faithful are never reconciled to God without the gift of regeneration; nay, we are for this end justified, —that we may afterwards serve God in holiness of life."[127] Then Calvin emphasized the fact that sanctification flows from and confirms justification.

Calvin accords justification a primary place: he saw it "the main hinge on which religion turns."[128] Pardon of sins and the imputed righteousness of Christ are the spring from which good works flow rather than are hindered.[129] Calvin saw that sanctification flows from our tasting the love of God we experienced in justification. In his explanation on the two benefits applied to us through the grace of Jesus Christ, he says,

---

124. Gleason, *John Calvin and John Owen*, 58.
125. Calvin, *Inst.* 2.5.14.
126. Gleason, *John Calvin and John Owen*, 58.
127. Calvin, *Calvin's Commentaries*, Rom 6:2.
128. Calvin, *Inst.* 3.11.1.
129. Hawkes, "Pious Pastors," 34.

One is remission of sins, which gives us assurance of salvation and peace of conscience; if this is our foundation, we may call God our Father. . . . God overlooks our unworthiness and accepts us because he sees the obedience of the Lord Jesus Christ. . . . But there is also a second. . . . Although, I say, we are in such a condition, the Lord Jesus Christ grants us grace so that we may seek what is good, and detest our sins. For as long as we remain in our sinful state, we seem to boast and revel in our fleshiness. But when once we have tasted the inestimable love of our God, and known the Lord Jesus Christ, we become so affected by his Holy Spirit that we condemn evil and seek to draw nearer to God in conformity to his holy will.[130]

Justification, Sanctification and the Glory of God

For Calvin, the glory of God is the ultimate aim to which our lives should be dedicated. The centrality of the glory of God was clear in Calvin's writings. Sometimes naturally when we think of the final cause of salvation, we choose the redemption of sinful persons; but this was not the final cause for Calvin. Calvin saw that "unmerited love of God" for the sinners is the first cause for salvation.[131] But as for the final cause, Calvin saw that "the apostle testifies that it consists both in the proof of divine justice and in the praise of God's goodness."[132]

Therefore, for Calvin, justification in itself is not an end but it is inseparable from sanctification by which our lives are transformed in conformity to Christ. Being conformed to Christ means being in full dedication to God and to his will that is glorifying his name. Under a title of "the sum of the Christian life" Calvin writes the following: "Now the great thing is this: we are consecrated and dedicated to God in order that we may thereafter think, speak, meditate, and do, nothing except to his glory."[133] Justification cannot be separated from sanctification because the aim is God's glory. In Calvin's thought, "the glory of God is the highest end, to which our sanctification is subordinate."[134]

---

130. Calvin, *Sermons on Galatians*, 198.
131. Calvin, *Calvin's Commentaries*, John 3:16.
132. Calvin, *Inst.* 3.14.17.
133. Calvin, *Inst.* 3.7.1.
134. Calvin, *Calvin's Commentaries*, Eph 1:4.

Moreover, Calvin emphasized that both justification and sanctification are the work of God and both of them are gifts of God's grace revealed in Jesus Christ through faith. This truth leaves the believer thankful, humble, in a position then to receive from Christ even more grace and giving more praise to God for saving him to the end. According to Calvin—the pastor and the theologian—justification, sanctification, piety and the glory of God are strongly interwoven. "*Pietas*, for the Genevan Pastor, was the *nexus* holding together orthodoxy and orthopraxy illustrated in a life of doxology."[135]

---

135. Gwin, "Mind and Heart Aflame," 3.

CHAPTER 2

The Westminster Standards
The Relation between Justification and Sanctification

Marshall's early life coincides with the era of the Westminster Assembly. We know that Marshall consulted two of the Westminster divines; Richard Baxter and Thomas Goodwin, in his struggle to grasp the power of the gospel for a holy life. This chapter aims to investigate the way the Westminster Assembly understood justification, sanctification and their relationship to each other. The debates that occurred at the Assembly about these issues are quite relevant to Marshall's ideas, putting in mind that the same dangers and errors were faced by both.

The dangers that were facing the church at the time of the Westminster Assembly are not different from what the church is facing today and from what the church has been facing from the very beginning. On one hand the divines were facing the danger of legalism or Neonomianism in which the gospel is presented as a new law the requirements of which are faith and repentance. On the other hand, they were facing the danger of Antinomianism in which believers are not obligated to the moral law anymore. Human beings are swinging between these two errors, moving from a carnal obedience of the law to the denial of any obligation of the law. A proper understanding of justification and sanctification and how they relate to one another is essential in addressing the two errors of Neonomianism and Antinomianism. The aim of this chapter is to discuss the relation between justification and sanctification in the light of the Westminster

Standards so that a proper understanding of this relationship will challenge these two errors.

Justification

The doctrine of justification has been a subject of much controversy and confusion through the ages. J. V. Fesko argues that "this doctrine has been called the material principle of the Reformation."[1] Anthony Burgess (d. 1664) who was one of the Westminster Divines, wrote, "It is very necessary to keep this [Justification] pure, because of the manifold truths that must fall if this fall; if you erre in this, the whole truth about Original sin, Freewill, and obligation of the Law will likewise perish."[2] Thomas Watson (1620-68) wrote a book which was published in 1692, "which followed the question and answer format of the *Westminster Shorter Catechism*."[3] Watson asserted that "justification is the very hinge and pillar of Christianity."[4] During the time of the Westminster Assembly, many errors about justification existed, and these same errors still exist today in many churches. The doctrine of justification is explained in chapter 11 in the *Confession*, in questions 70-71 in the *Larger Catechism* and in question 33 in the *Shorter Catechism*. The *Catechisms* are clear in their refutation of the Roman Catholic and Arminian views. The *Confession* resonates with what the *Catechisms* say about justification; it refutes on one hand the Roman Catholic and Arminian doctrines of justification (11.1), and on the other hand it refutes the Antinomian doctrines of justification (11.2).

The Roman Catholic doctrine of justification teaches that God infuses righteousness into us, and then declares us righteous because he actually makes us righteous.[5] This teaching is asserted in the Council of Trent: "Justification is not only a remission of sins but also the sanctification and renewal of the inward man through the voluntary reception of the grace and gifts whereby an unjust man becomes just and from being an enemy becomes a friend."[6] While the Arminian teachers believe that faith itself is

---

1. Fesko, *Theology of the Westminster Standards*, 207.
2. Burgess, *True Doctrine of Justification*, 3.
3. Beeke and Pederson, *Meet the Puritans*, 608.
4. Watson, *Body of Divinity*, 226.
5. Van Dixhoorn, *Confessing the Faith*, 160.
6. Schroeder, *Canons and Decrees*, sixth session, 7.33.

imputed to us for righteousness.[7] In response, the Westminster Assembly emphasized two realities about justification. First, justification is a law-word which is borrowed from courts of justice among men.[8] Justification is a judicial word with all the expressions connected to it like "condemnation" as its opposite, our sins which are called "debts," and Christ who is called our "Advocate" denote a judiciary proceeding.[9] Therefore, to be justified does not mean that one is made righteous nor that an inward change has happened so that the person becomes inherently righteous. Thomas Watson contends that "God, in justifying a person, pronounces him to be righteous, and looks upon him as if he had not sinned."[10] In his exposition of the theology of the Assembly, Robert Letham says, "thus, justification is *forensic*, by the imputation or accounting of Christ's righteousness, not *renovative* by the impartation or infusion of grace, as Rome taught."[11] To say that justification is by infusion of grace is to conflate justification and sanctification. As the *Confession* and the *Larger Catechism* teach, justification does not depend on "anything wrought in them or done by them." The justified receive and rest on Christ for justification by faith. Watson comments on this idea by saying that "the dignity is not in faith as a grace, but relatively, as it lays hold on Christ's merits."[12]

The second reality about justification that the Assembly highlights in order to argue against the Roman Catholic and Arminian claims is the freeness and gracious nature of justification. Burgess says that in justification is the grace and good favor of God especially revealed.[13] We find a clear emphasis in the *Confession*, *Shorter Catechism*, and *Larger Catechism* on the freeness of God's act of justifying the sinners. In the three documents, Rom 3:24 ("Being justified *as a gift* by his grace") is used as an exegetical foundation. "Justification is a mercy spun out of the bowels of free grace."[14] If justification was not out of totally free grace having nothing to do with our own righteousness, then we would never be secure. Truly, God makes us increasingly righteous in this life, but this process is called sanctification

---

7. Arminius, *Works of James Arminius*, 50n.
8. Fisher and Erskine, *Westminster Assembly's Shorter Catechism Explained*, 175.
9. Burgess, *True Doctrine of Justification*, 8.
10. Watson, *Body of Divinity*, 227.
11. Letham, *Westminster Assembly*, 270.
12. Watson, *Body of Divinity*, 227.
13. Burgess, *True Doctrine of Justification*, 3.
14. Watson, *Body of Divinity*, 227.

which is never complete in this life. Therefore, one can never depend on something incomplete in order to stand righteous before a just God.[15]

The Ground of Justification

The gracious nature of justification raises some questions. The first question is, "How can it stand with God's justice and holiness to pronounce us innocent when we are guilty?"[16] The Westminster Assembly's answer to this question is "For Christ's sake alone." Because Christ made satisfaction for our sins, "God may, in equity and justice, pronounce us righteous."[17] Therefore, the foundation of this justification is as solid and firm as any rock, it being the righteousness of Christ.[18] Another question raised is "How can free grace be the moving cause of our justification, when it is 'through the redemption that is in Christ Jesus'?"[19] The Assembly's answer was that "through the imputation of the obedience and satisfaction of Christ unto them [the believers or the elect], they receive and rest on Him and His righteousness by faith" (11.1).

Justification Debate

In this area of the ground of justification, "the initial discussions in the Assembly were marked by intense debates."[20] However, the main controversy regarding justification had to do with whether the active obedience of Christ is imputed to the one justified by faith. This discussion took place from session 47 (Wednesday, 6th of September 1643) to session 52 (Tuesday 12th of September 1643).[21] The two chief parties in these discussions debated around the imputation of the active obedience of Christ.[22]

Divines like Thomas Gataker (1577–1654) and Richard Vines (1599–1656) were among those who refused that the active obedience of

---

15. Van Dixhoorn, *Confessing the Faith*, 160.
16. Watson, *Body of Divinity*, 227.
17. Watson, *Body of Divinity*, 227.
18. Burgess, *True Doctrine of Justification*, 10.
19. Fisher and Erskine, *Westminster Assembly's Shorter Catechism Explained*, 176.
20. Fesko, *Theology of the Westminster Standards*, 209.
21. Letham, *Westminster Assembly*, 253.
22. Fesko, *Theology of the Westminster Standards*, 210.

Christ was imputed to us for justification.[23] Although Gataker and Vines were united in their position to deny the imputation of active obedience of Christ, yet they were different in some areas.[24] According to Letham, Vines argued that "justification consisted solely in the remission of sins in which our justification is connected to the sufferings and blood of Christ."[25] Vines said, "That which stickes with me: it hath seemed very much suiting[?] with the face of the whole scriptures to assigne our Justification, taking it for the remission of sins, to the passive obedience of Christ."[26] On the other hand, "Gataker argued that Christ's passive obedience was imputed and the remission of sins was something separate, following justification."[27] Chad Van Dixhoorn argues that "the majority of the divines included forgiveness within justification, which is similar to Vines' position; but they also saw in justification the imputation of the righteousness of Christ."[28] However, Vines and Gataker both agreed to refuse the idea of the imputation of Christ's obedience for justification.

According to the views of this party, "Christ needed to fulfill the law in order to be a perfect sacrifice."[29] Vines argued, "For Christs[sic] purity of nature, you will not say that is imputed for justification & soe[sic] for those acts of obedience as pure man. All doth some way conduce as the lambe[sic] must be without spot, but it is not that which makes it a sacrifice but bloud[sic]."[30] Christ had to fulfill the law for his own sake, because He was man in relation to God. Gataker asserted "The takin[sic] of Christs[sic] humanity to subsist together with his deity in one person doth not excuse the human nature of Christ to cease to be a creature, & then Christ as man did owe a duty to God his creator."[31] Furthermore, this party argued that the Scripture attributed redemption and reconciliation to Christ's blood, not to his obedience. Vines argued

> That which stickes with me: it hath seemed very much suiting [?] with the face of the whole scriptures to assigne our Justification,

---

23. Letham, *Westminster Assembly*, 253.
24. Fesko, *Theology of the Westminster Standards*, 210.
25. Letham, *Westminster Assembly*, 253.
26. Van Dixhoorn et al., *Minutes and Papers*, 2:53.
27. Letham, *Westminster Assembly*, 253.
28. Van Dixhoorn, "Strange Silence of Prolocutor Twisse," 409.
29. Letham, *Westminster Assembly*, 255.
30. Van Dixhoorn et al., *Minutes and Papers*, 2:53.
31. Van Dixhoorn et al., *Minutes and Papers*, 2:54.

taking it for the remissions of sins, to the passive obedience of Christ.... The passive sufferings of Christ the proper matter imputed. "Making peace". "Redeemed by his bloud". "Set forth in bloud". "Without bloud noe[sic] remission". "Bloud of Christ purgeth us from all sin".[32]

Then he further argued on the next day, "That which the legall[sic] purgings & expiations in the time of the law did foresignify was bloud[sic] and that was necessary to be. That which purgeth all sin & leaves none, that is our righteousnesse. 'But the bloud of Christ...'."[33]

Letham asserts that "the majority of the Assembly held that Christ's active obedience was imputed for justification."[34] Among those who offered many speeches for the imputation of the active obedience of Christ were Joshua Hoyle (d. 1654), Thomas Goodwin (1600–1680), Lazarus Seaman (d. 1675), William Gouge (1575–1653), Daniel Featley (1582–1645) and George Walker (1581–1651).[35] The latter used Scriptural evidence such as Isa 54:14; 61:10; Pss 24:5; and 69 to argue that the sons of God have righteousness that they cannot possess by their own works and duties of sanctification, and that this righteousness can only be achieved through the active obedience of Christ.[36]

Goodwin had several arguments for the imputation of Christ's active obedience. He referred to the contrast between Adam's sin and Christ's obedience in Rom 5:12–19 in which Christ's fulfillment of the law is intended, and not only his death. He argued, "From the opposition betweene Adams sin & Jesus Christ's obedience: Adams sin is called 'one disobedience' & 'of one man' but 17 v. oppositely to this one sin, 'abundance of grace'. If passive obedience only meant, that was but one offering, but this hath many parts of righteousnesse[sic]."[37] Goodwin also contended that Christ was not obliged to keep the law but that "He took it [our nature] to noe other end but that he might save and Justify us."[38] Therefore, Christ's subjecting himself to the law was more than that of a creature under the law. Goodwin clarified "The maine[sic] subject [of this obedience] is the person, therefore

---

32. Van Dixhoorn et al., *Minutes and Papers*, 2:53.
33. Van Dixhoorn et al., *Minutes and Papers*, 2:61.
34. Letham, *Westminster Assembly*, 253.
35. Fesko, *Theology of the Westminster Standards*, 210, 214.
36. Van Dixhoorn et al., *Minutes and Papers*, 2:62.
37. Van Dixhoorn et al., *Minutes and Papers*, 2:63–64.
38. Van Dixhoorn et al., *Minutes and Papers*, 2:64.

called the 'bloud of God'."[39] Regarding the centrality of the blood of Christ and how it is strongly tied to redemption and reconciliation in the Scriptural language, Goodwin commented that "The reason is because the last part of the pount & the great peril of it. It is true, 'without bloud noe remission'. The active obedience would not save us without this."[40] Another proponent for the imputation of Christ's active obedience was Featley. He argued that Christ was not only obeying the law as a private person but also as a public person who was representing others.[41] He also argued that when the Scripture bears upon the passive obedience of Christ for justification, this usage is "*synekdocke*" where the passive did merit the imputation of his active.[42]

One of the most important concerns for those who deny the imputation of the active obedience of Christ is Antinomianism. "Both Vines and Gataker were strongly anti-antinomian. They feared that the inclusion of the active obedience of Christ in justification would lead in that direction, since believers has no reason to be obliged to follow the moral law."[43] Featley answered the objection by saying that "This doth not any way favour them, because his [Christ's] obedience is only imputed to penitent sinners."[44] Woodcock also expressed his fears of Antinomianism. He argued that if the active obedience of Christ is imputed to us, then a merit is intrinsically included in God's children, "Then God can see noe sin in his children."[45] Accordingly, justified persons would be free from the requirement to obey the law. Walker answered saying that Woodcock's argument would be also valid for the imputation of the passive obedience of Christ.[46] In addition to that, Gouge argued that "God doth not looke upon us as having fulfilled the whole for ourselves, but by our suerty[*sic*], & therefore it is said 'acounted'."[47]

After much hot debate, they resolved that the wording should be "his whole obedience and satisfaction being by God imputed to us."[48] Session 52

---

39. Van Dixhoorn et al., *Minutes and Papers*, 2:64.
40. Van Dixhoorn et al., *Minutes and Papers*, 2:64.
41. Van Dixhoorn et al., *Minutes and Papers*, 2:72.
42. Van Dixhoorn et al., *Minutes and Papers*, 2: 73.
43. Letham, *Westminster Assembly*, 263.
44. Van Dixhoorn et al., *Minutes and Papers*, 2:95–96.
45. Van Dixhoorn et al., *Minutes and Papers*, 2:82.
46. Van Dixhoorn et al., *Minutes and Papers*, 2:82.
47. Van Dixhoorn et al., *Minutes and Papers*, 2:83.
48. Letham, *Westminster Assembly*, 261.

is closed with the sentence: "The Question was put 3 [or 4] only dissenting."[49] Fesko argues that "the phrase 'whole obedience' was intended to denote the imputation of both the active and passive obedience of Christ."[50] Although this statement was the outcome of the debate in 1643, the final wording of article 11 in the *Confession* neither included the statement "whole obedience" nor "active or passive obedience." The final language in the *Confession* is "obedience and satisfaction of Christ" and in the *Larger Catechism* a "perfect obedience and full satisfaction." Robert Letham argues that "the care the Assembly took over the phraseology indicates a desire to include all its members in accepting the statement."[51] Moreover, Fesko claims that "the absence of the old language 'the whole obedience' has led some to conclude that the assembly later accommodated the minority views of Gataker,"[52] or that "the imputation of the active obedience of Christ was viewed as a debatable matter but not a test of orthodoxy."[53] In support of this possibility is that when the Congregationalists led by Goodwin, one of the original Westminster divines, and John Owen adopted a modified version of the *Confession* in the *Savoy Declaration* (1658), they modified the chapter on justification.[54] The *Savoy Declaration* states that justification is "by imputing Christ's active obedience to the whole law, and passive obedience in his death for their whole and sole righteousness."[55] This explanation shows that the *Savoy Declaration* mentions intentionally the active and passive obedience of Christ, "as if to correct the undue flexibility and ambiguity at Westminster."[56]

Contrarily, other scholars like Jeffrey K. Jue and Carl R. Trueman believe that "a holistic view of the Westminster Standards shows that the divines continued to believe in the imputation of Christ's active obedience for justification."[57] Among the arguments, "the series of *Larger Catechism* questions on the humiliation of Christ (qq. 46–50) distinguish between Christ's

---

49. Van Dixhoorn et al., *Minutes and Papers*, 2:107.
50. Fesko, *Theology of the Westminster Standards*, 217.
51. Letham, *Westminster Assembly*, 262.
52. Fesko, *Theology of the Westminster Standards*, 217.
53. Fesko, *Theology of the Westminster Standards*, 224.
54. Fesko, *Theology of the Westminster Standards*, 224.
55. *Savoy Declaration*, chapter 11.
56. Letham, *Westminster Assembly*, 262.
57. Fesko, *Theology of the Westminster Standards*, 224n.

perfect fulfillment of the law (q. 48) and Christ's death (qq. 49-50)."⁵⁸ Also the original statement in the *Confession* in 11.3 separates the two aspects of Christ's work by a comma (his obedience, and death) which reflects the active and passive obedience of Christ. Moreover, the phrase "obedience and satisfaction" was used in the literature of the period to refer to the active and passive obedience of Christ.⁵⁹ One of the evidences of such use is present in George Walker's defense of the doctrine of justification, "who offered twenty-four speeches in the assembly in favor for the imputation of the active obedience of Christ."⁶⁰

Eternal Justification

The fear of Antinomianism was not only connected to the imputation of the active obedience of Christ but also to the doctrine of justification from eternity. "The idea of a justification in eternity is the intellectual starting point for a number of key tenets of Antinomianism."⁶¹ Fesko explains the Antinomian view as he says that "They believed that God not only decrees justification but also justifies the elect in eternity through Christ's work; hence, when a person comes to faith, that awakening is not the moment of his justification but rather the discovery of his justified status."⁶² Letham contends that "the crucial center of gravity of justification for Antinomians was the eternal decree and the historical accomplishment of Christ."⁶³ This view was not far from the views of even some members in the Westminster Assembly. "William Twisse (1578–1646), the assembly's first prolocutor, held to this doctrine."⁶⁴ The result was that "the antinomians conflated the *accomplishment* of redemption with the *application* of redemption."⁶⁵

The Assembly rejected the idea of "justification from eternity" clearly in its documents. The language articulated in the *Confession* keeps the balance between the sovereign decree of God and the application of salvation to

---

58. Fesko, *Theology of the Westminster Standards*, 225.
59. Fesko, *Theology of the Westminster Standards*, 227.
60. Fesko, *Theology of the Westminster Standards*, 227–28.
61. Van Dixhoorn, "Strange Silence of Prolocutor Twisse," 403.
62. Fesko, *Theology of the Westminster Standards*, 229.
63. Letham, *Westminster Assembly*, 272.
64. Fesko, *Theology of the Westminster Standards*, 229.
65. Van Dixhoorn, "Strange Silence of Prolocutor Twisse," 405. Italics are mine.

the elect in history:[66] "God did, from all eternity, decree to justify the elect, and Christ did, in the fullness of time, die for their sins, and rise again for their justification: nevertheless, they are not justified until the Holy Spirit does, in due time, actually apply Christ unto them" (11.4). G. I. Williamson comments on the Assembly's teaching, "It is true that God foreordained the justification of the elect, and it is true that God provided the basis for justification in the finished work of Christ, yet the actual application of such to men is distinct from it."[67] "To deny the reality of justification as an occurrence in the life of a person is most unhelpful and does not account for the emphasis of Holy Scripture itself."[68] Burgess, argued against eternal justification by saying that "the Scripture speaks of state of wrath that all are in before they become justified."[69] He adds "if a person before regeneration and conversion is a child of wrath under guilt and punishment of sin, then he could not be at the same time in the favour of God, and at peace with him."[70] Watson argues that the idea of "justification from eternity" is false because "by nature we are under a sentence of condemnation (John 3:18) and we could never have been condemned if we were justified from eternity."[71] Moreover, "the divines countered this position as they believed that it would undermine the doctrine of sanctification."[72] Watson affirms how justification from eternity could undermine the doctrine of sanctification by the following words:

> Justification is to those who believe and repent. Therefore, their sins were uncancelled, and their persons unjustified till they did repent. Though God does not justify us for our repentance, yet not without it. The Antinomians erroneously hold, that we are justified from eternity. This doctrine is a key which opens the door to all licentiousness; for what sins do they care not to commit, so long as they hold they are justified whether they repent or not?[73]

---

66. Letham, *Westminster Assembly*, 272.
67. Williamson, *Westminster Confession of Faith*, 141–42.
68. Van Dixhoorn, *Confessing the Faith*, 168.
69. Burgess, *True Doctrine of Justification*, 169–70.
70. Burgess, *True Doctrine of Justification*, 170.
71. Watson, *Body of Divinity*, 228.
72. Letham, *Westminster Assembly*, 272.
73. Watson, *Body of Divinity*, 228.

Justification by Faith

When Antinomians are asked about the role of faith in justification, their answer would be that faith is only a manifestation of justification which already happened in eternity.[74] Burgess describes the antinomian view of faith and repentance as follows: "They make faith not instrumentall[sic] cause to apply pardon, but only a perswasion[sic] that sinne[sic] is pardoned; and thus repentance shall not be a *condition* to qualifie[sic] the subject, to obtain forgivenesse[sic], but a *sign* to manifest that sin is forgiven."[75] This Antinomian teaching was a technique to fight back against "the Arminian understanding of faith that made it a new "work" in the covenant of grace."[76] The Antinomians wanted to avoid any hint of contribution from man's side in his justification. Therefore, they considered faith as a mere recognition of eternal justification. The Westminster Assembly clearly resisted this teaching while revising the article about justification in session 46 on September 5th, 1643.[77]

On the other hand, the Arminian view of faith and its role in justification was also rejected by the Assembly. Arminius believed that a person is not justified by the imputed righteousness of Christ; rather the act of believing itself is accounted as our justifying righteousness. Therefore, God looks upon the sinner's faith as righteousness and God is willing to do this because of Christ's obedience. Arminius comments on the language "we are justified by faith":

> I deny that this expression is figurative, *We are justified by faith,* that is, by the thing which faith apprehends. Neither am I pleased with the following interpretation of the phrase, which is used the first of all in this subject, *Abraham believed God, and it was imputed unto him for righteousness,* that is that which Abraham apprehends by faith, is imputed to him for righteousness. For not *the object which he apprehends by faith,* but *his believing,* is said to be imputed to him for righteousness: From which St. Paul has chosen his phrase, *Faith is imputed for righteousness.*[78]

---

74. Van Dixhoorn, "Strange Silence of Prolocutor Twisse," 405–6.
75. Burgess, *True Doctrine of Justification,* 169. Italics his.
76. Van Dixhoorn, "Strange Silence of Prolocutor Twisse," 405.
77. Van Dixhoorn et al., *Minutes and Papers,* 2:43–47.
78. Arminius, *Works of James Arminius,* 2:50n.

For Arminius, justification occurs on the basis of faith and not by or through faith, whereby faith is foundational for justification and not instrumental.[79] The Westminster Assembly clearly resisted the Arminian view of faith in relation to justification. We note that the Assembly was clear about the role of faith in our justification. In the *Confession* (11.1), the *Larger Catechism* (Q 70) and the *Shorter Catechism* (Q 33), the instrumentality of faith is clearly expressed by the preposition "by." Chad Van Dixhoorn comments on the meaning of faith in the Confession (11.2), "Faith is not some kind of virtue in us but rather it is receiving and resting on Christ alone."[80] In 11.1, the *Confession* is clear in rejecting the Arminian view, as it says that "nor by imputing faith itself, the act of believing, or any other evangelical obedience to them, as their righteousness." The *Confession* uses the word "instrument" to emphasize the role of faith in justification as the hand or instrument which receives the righteousness of Christ.

Moreover, faith is not only described as an instrument but as the sole instrument of justification. This language is directed against the error of the Romanists who hold that hope, and love, and repentance are included in faith as justifying, and concur with faith, strictly so called, to justification.[81] In the second paragraph in the *Confession* concerning justification (11.2), the Roman Catholic doctrine of justification is clearly refuted. The Roman Catholic view confounds justification with sanctification and represents justification as the infusion of righteousness into the souls of men. On the other hand, "the Westminster Standards teach that the sole basis of God's justifying act is found in what is termed *the righteousness*, or as in the *Larger Catechism*, *the perfect obedience and the full satisfaction* of Christ whose satisfaction was proper, real and complete."[82] Therefore, "faith is the only instrument of justification because Christ is its only ground."[83]

The Assembly was quite keen to refuse any Roman or Arminian notion that man contributes in any sense to his own justification and this includes faith itself. However, the divines argued against the Antinomians by saying that actual justification happens in the life of Christians by the instrumentality of faith. They added that this faith is not alone in the person justified, but that it works with love (11.2). The godly life for the justified

79. Fesko, *Theology of the Westminster Standards*, 219–20.
80. Van Dixhoorn, *Confessing the Faith*, 163–64.
81. Shaw, *Reformed Faith*, 182.
82. Morris, *Theology of the Westminster Symbols*, 439.
83. Letham, *Westminster Assembly*, 271.

person was an inevitable reality. Faith is the sole gift of grace by which we receive justification, "but this one saving grace is accompanied by all other saving graces (11.2)."[84] The Assembly used James 2:17, 22, 26 as a proof text in 11.2 to say that the faith that does not work with love (Gal 5:6) is dead. Faith never exists alone, but is always accompanied and bears holy fruit in the life. However, it alone, and no other grace is the instrument of uniting us to Christ, and so of effecting our justification.[85]

A Need for Balance

From what has preceded, we see that the divines were trying to keep a very important balance. They did not want to undermine the doctrine of sanctification, so they avoided any notion of Antinomianism that may occur because of the teaching of eternal justification or, as some have suggested, through the imputation of the active obedience of Christ. They believed that such teachings remove any urgency from man to repent and exercise faith. They emphasized that man is actually justified when he exercises faith in Christ. On the other hand, the divines refuted Arminianism or Roman Catholicism which give great weight to man's contribution to his own salvation. Therefore, for them, faith was the only instrument by which man receives and rests on Christ and his righteousness for justification.

Finding this balance was not an easy task. We have seen that in order to avoid the danger of Antinomianism, the divines debated whether "the satisfaction rendered by Christ to law and justice was provided by his passive obedience, his vicarious sufferings and death only, or was provided by his comprehensive obedience, active as well as passive, exhibited throughout His mediatorial career."[86] Another example of a divine who had great concern over Antinomianism was John Lightfoot (1602–75), "whose opinions are not recorded in the minutes."[87] Lightfoot had some concerns on using the phrase "accounted righteous" as the word "accounted" was close to an Antinomian interpretation of eternal justification. Instead, "he favored the phrase 'made and accounted righteous,' apparently oblivious to the probability that this would be even closer to the Roman Catholic view."[88]

---

84. Van Dixhoorn, *Confessing the Faith*, 164.
85. Hodge and Hodge, *System of Theology*, 65.
86. Morris, *Theology of the Westminster Symbols*, 440.
87. Van Dixhoorn, "Strange Silence of Prolocutor Twisse," 413.
88. Letham, *Westminster Assembly*, 253.

Van Dixhoorn comments on this saying, "Concern over Antinomianism had risen to such a pitch that a handful of divines, Lightfoot included, were willing to sacrifice soteriological clarity and anti-Catholic polemic on the altar of anti-nomianism."[89] On the other end we find that "the Antinomians were anti-Arminian to an extreme."[90] Van Dixhoorn goes on to argue that "Twisse, was one who among others combated Arminianism by positing a justification in eternity."[91]

The Assembly succeeded to keep the balance between these two errors, Neonomianism in its Roman Catholica or Arminian form on the one side, and Antinomianism on the other end. If one side is blurring the distinctions between justification and sanctification, the other side sacrifices sanctification on the altar of justification. The divines were concerned to distinguish justification from sanctification (against Roman Catholicism), and to deny any notion that man has a kind of quality which qualifies him to be justified (against Arminianism). In order to achieve that end, the union with Christ is strongly highlighted.

Union with Christ

One of the most important principles in the minds of the divines that keeps the balance mentioned above and keeps justification and sanctification as distinct yet inseparable is union with Christ. Some claim that the Assembly held union with Christ in an inseparable relation with sanctification but not with justification. Thomas F. Torrance argues that "the Confession did not take the line of Calvin and the Scots Reformation theology in which justification and union with Christ are held inseparably together."[92] It is true that chapter 11 in the *Confession* did not contain the word "union" with Christ, but does this mean that the divines did not hold justification and union with Christ as inseparable?

One of the divines who was greatly involved in the debates over justification was George Walker. "His main interest was union with Christ."[93] Van Dixhoorn contends that "Walker's soteriology, resonated with Calvin, emphasized the believer's union with Christ, and he wrote more about this

---

89. Van Dixhoorn, "Strange Silence of Prolocutor Twisse," 413.
90. Van Dixhoorn, "Strange Silence of Prolocutor Twisse," 405n.
91. Van Dixhoorn, "Strange Silence of Prolocutor Twisse," 405.
92. Torrance, *Scottish Theology*, 144.
93. Letham, *Westminster Assembly*, 252.

subject than many of his fellow divines."[94] In one of his speeches during the discussion of the doctrine of justification in the Assembly (Session 46) he said the following words, "God by that Spirit by which he doth unite us unto Christ, he doth worke faith on us, make us new creatures. Now when thus united unto Christ, we actually apply Christ with all his benefitts[sic] & soe we come to be justifyed[sic], to lay hold upon Christ, injoy & possesse[sic] Christ & soe have a fruitive or possessive justification."[95] Walker's words show that justification and union with Christ are inseparable.

Walker's view on the relation between justification and union with Christ was not just a personal view. The Assembly also held the same view, and this appears in the *Confession* and the *Larger Catechism*. Chapter 11 in the *Confession* begins with referring to the close connection between justification and effectual calling: "Those whom God effectually calls, he also freely justifies." In the Assembly's mind, those who are justified are those who are effectually called. The effectual calling is "God's grace to His elect by which he powerfully and graciously draws them to Christ by the Holy Spirit (10.1)."[96] Therefore, God by his effectual gracious call draws his elect to Christ to be justified. The inseparable connection between justification and union with Christ is even clearer in the *Larger Catechism*. Question 69 says, "What is the communion in grace which the members of the invisible church have with Christ?" The answer is, "The communion in grace which the members of the invisible church have with Christ, is their partaking of the virtue of his mediation, in their justification, adoption, sanctification and whatever else, in this life, manifests their union with him." Joseph Morecraft writes, "The *Catechism* begins its exposition of the application of salvation to the believer with a statement about the believer's *communion in grace with Christ* from which relationship flows all the blessings of salvation into their lives, including justification and sanctification."[97] The proof text used to support this answer is 1 Cor 1:30 which emphasized that being united to Christ "in Christ," God made Christ to us "wisdom, and righteous, and sanctification, and redemption." All these evidences show that the Assembly believed and taught an inseparable relation between union with Christ and justification.

---

94. Van Dixhoorn, "Strange Silence of Prolocutor Twisse," 414.
95. Van Dixhoorn et al., *Minutes and Papers*, 2:45.
96. Letham, *Westminster Assembly*, 269.
97. Morecraft, *Authentic Christianity*, 2:723.

Justification and Sanctification

Sanctification is also strongly attached to union with Christ in the Westminster Standards. What we already have seen in question 69 in the *Larger Catechism* regarding justification also applies to sanctification. In the *Confession*, although the word "union" is not stated in chapter 13, it is implied. First of all, the chapter begins similarly to the chapter on justification with a reference to the effectual calling by which we are drawn to Christ. Secondly, one of the proof texts used is Rom 6:5–6 that refers directly to union with Christ as the only way to be dead to sin. Van Dixhoorn argues that for the Assembly, "sanctification was found in union with Christ, like every Christian blessing and benefit."[98]

The Westminster Assembly resembled Calvin's view on the inseparability of justification and sanctification that the believers have in Christ. Calvin expressed their inseparability saying, "But, since the question concerns only righteousness and sanctification, let us dwell upon these. Although we may distinguish them, Christ contains both of them inseparably in himself."[99] The Assembly debated the question "What is sanctification?" for four sessions until the final wording was approved in session 855.[100] They discussed the relation between justification and sanctification which is answered in Question 77 in the *Larger Catechism* in session 852.[101] Being clear in answering this question was extremely important for the Assembly in arguing against Neonomianism and Antinomianism in their time and is also important in our time now.

Morecraft asserts that, "although Question 77 in the *Larger Catechism* is concerned with the differences between justification and sanctification, it begins by emphasizing that they are also inseparably joined."[102] The proof texts used for the inseparability are 1 Cor 6:11 and 1:30. This beginning is important for two reasons. First, it shows the error of Antinomianism that says that since we are forgiven by free grace, we have no obligation to keep the law whatsoever. In Question 76, the Assembly asserts that being forgiven by grace (justified) means that the person by God's grace through the Spirit of God endeavors constantly to walk with God in all the ways

---

98. Van Dixhoorn, *Confessing the Faith*, 178.
99. Calvin, *Inst.* 3.16.1.
100. Bower, *Larger Catechism*, 30n.
101. Van Dixhoorn et al., *Minutes and Papers*, 4:570.
102. Morecraft, *Authentic Christianity*, 3:172.

of new obedience. The proof texts given for this walking with God in new obedience are Ps 119:5, 59, 128; Luke 1:6; and 2 Kgs 23:25 and all of them refer to obeying God's law. Then in Question 77 the divines emphasize the inseparability of justification of sanctification before clarifying the difference between them. Secondly, Question 77 answers the Roman Catholic's claim that Protestants hold that men continuing in sin are justified. As Watson writes, "Righteous imputed for justification and righteous inherent for sanctification must be inseparably united."[103] He goes on to say on the inseparability of justification and sanctification:

> Holiness indeed is not the cause of our justification, but it is the attendant; as the heat in the sun is not the cause of its light, but it is the attendant; it is absurd to imagine that God should justify a people, and they should still go on in sin. If God should justify a people and not sanctify them, he would justify a people whom he could not glorify.[104]

The Assembly was also careful to distinguish between justification and sanctification in Question 77. Confusing justification and sanctification would lead to the Roman Catholic doctrine of justification by self-righteousness.[105] The *Larger Catechism* points out three main differences between justification and sanctification. First, in justification God imputes the righteousness of Christ to us and so we are accepted; in sanctification the Spirit infuses grace in us and enables us to live righteously. Secondly, in justification sin is pardoned because of Christ (Rom 3:24–25); in sanctification sin is subdued because of Christ (Rom 6:6, 14). Thirdly, in justification all believers are *equally* freed from the revenging wrath of God in a *perfect* way now in this life that they never fall into condemnation (Rom 8:1); but in sanctification the believers are not sanctified to the same degree and their sanctification is never perfect in this life. True believers are growing towards perfection which is a lifelong process completed only at death (Phil 3:12–14). Therefore, the Assembly held that justification is different from sanctification—a position against Roman Catholicism and Neonomianism in general; "but they also held that without sanctification we have no evidence for our justification"[106]—a position against Antinomianism.

---

103. Watson, *Body of Divinity*, 229.
104. Watson, *Body of Divinity*, 229.
105. Morecraft, *Authentic Christianity*, 3:172.
106. Watson, *Body of Divinity*, 244.

The Westminster Standards

Not Only Inseparable but Dependent

Thus, the Assembly maintained an inseparable relationship between justification and sanctification and that both are tied to the union with Christ. Moreover, a logical relationship can be seen between justification and sanctification in the Westminster Standards. Fesko argues that "sanctification is not foundational to justification but subsequent to it in the *Confession's* treatment of salvation."[107] Burgess argues that justification and sanctification are conjoined together "so that although there be a priority of nature" for justification, yet they are together in time.[108] James Fisher (1679–1775) while commenting on Question 35 in the *Shorter Catechism* "What is Sanctification?" says that "although justification and sanctification as to time are simultaneous; yet, as to the order of nature, justification goes before sanctification, as the cause before the effect, or as fire is before light and heat."[109] Samuel Rutherford (1600–1661), one of the Scottish commissioners to the Assembly, believed that justification causes sanctification. Rutherford was arguing against the Antinomians, "who claimed that sanctification makes men saints declaratively to men-ward where justification makes them saints in the sight of God."[110] He argued,

> But take Sanctification for holy walking in the strength of the grace of justification, and grace inherent in us; so we say, Justification and Sanctification ought not to bee separated, but both concurre to make us Saints; the one as the cause, the other as the unseparable effect.[111]

Walker commented about how justification makes a difference in our lives by saying that "when we are justifyed by faith, if at any time Sathan[sic] tempt us, then by faith we fly to the righteousness of Christ . . . then we go on & show our fruites."[112] Walker argued that being justified enables us to fight Satan by running to God and therefore bear fruits. Without justification we are condemned sinners in the sight of the Lord and we are not accepted so how can we ask God to grant us to fight sin?

---

107. Fesko, *Theology of the Westminster Standards*, 251.
108. Burgess, *True Doctrine of Justification*, 172.
109. Fisher and Erskine, *Westminster Assembly's Shorter Catechism Explained*, 188.
110. Rutherford, *Survey of the Spirituall Antichrist*, 155.
111. Rutherford, *Survey of the Spirituall Antichrist*, 155.
112. Van Dixhoorn et al., *Minutes and Papers*, 2:45.

According to the Westminster Standards, justification has two elements: pardon of all our sins and our acceptance as righteous in the sight of God (*WCF* 11.1; *WLC* 70; *WSC* 33) and this by imputing Christ's obedience and satisfaction unto those who receive and rest on him by faith. Therefore, what happens in justification is "a change of state, of condition and of relationship."[113] Naturally we are God's enemies, our sins have separated us from God, alienating us as sinners from him. We cannot receive the gifts of God and the inheritance of God's children unless we are first reconciled and be accepted with him. Reconciliation can only happen when our sins are forgiven. Moreover, "we must be given that by which we are accepted with God which is the righteousness of Christ."[114] Therefore, in the *Larger Catechism*, Question 69, "the first of those blessings of redemption in our communion in grace with Christ, which belongs to believers by virtue of our union with Christ and His accomplishments as our Mediator is justification."[115] Because in justification the believer is forgiven of his sins and clothed in the righteousness of Christ, "he is in a favorable position with God to receive all the gifts of God's love for His own people,"[116] including sanctification.

Moreover, the divines were very careful in the use of tenses in their expression of theological truths. Their use of tenses in the *Confession* reflects the logical order they held for justification and sanctification. In the beginning of chapter 11 on justification, they began with a reference to those whom God justifies using the phrase "Those whom God effectually calls." The divines used the present simple tense with the effectual calling. But in chapter 13 on sanctification, they referred to the same people using the phrase "They who are effectually called." This time the divines used the past tense with the effectual calling. These uses of tenses show that the divines believed that justification happens simultaneously with effectual calling and that sanctification follows that.[117]

This aggregation of evidences show that the divines articulated a clear inseparable relationship between justification and sanctification where

---

113. Morris, *Theology of the Westminster Symbols*, 444.
114. Morecraft, *Authentic Christianity*, 2:725.
115. Morecraft, *Authentic Christianity*, 2:724.
116. Morecraft, *Authentic Christianity*, 2:725.
117. The divines were careful in their use of tenses in the Westminster Standards. For instance, in the *Shorter Catechism*, they used the past tense in Question 27 while discussing Christ's humiliation but they used the present tense in Question 28 while discussing Christ's exaltation.

sanctification follows justification or even depends on it. These evidences also emphasize the reality that justification and sanctification were distinct blessings granted to those in communion with Christ.

Conclusion

In the context of Antinomianism and Neonomianism, and in the light of Arminian and Roman Catholic views of justification, the Westminster divines were very careful to distinguish between the complete judicial act of justification on the ground of Christ obedience and satisfaction alone which we receive by faith alone, and God's conforming our life to the image of Christ by his Spirit and his word throughout our lives, the process that is called sanctification. As Fesko states, "They believed that these two benefits were vital to the broader doctrine of salvation and held off the threats of Antinomianism and Neonomianism."[118] Union with Christ in his life, death, and resurrection was central to their theology through which all the blessings of redemption flow to the believers. The divines showed the errors of the two extremes of Antinomianism and Neonomianism by holding to the distinct, inseparable, logically arranged relationship of justification and sanctification.

---

118. Fesko, *Theology of the Westminster Standards*, 266.

CHAPTER 3

Marshall on Justification

The questions about salvation and how this salvation relates to holiness are always pressing questions. Therefore, much ink has been spilled in discussing sanctification and how it relates to our salvation. So far, we have seen that justification, sanctification, and their relation were very essential doctrines in the writings of John Calvin and in the Westminster standards. Any misconception about these doctrines would inevitably lead to serious errors. Andrew Murray of South Africa says, "There is but one book in the language admitted by all to be the standard one on 'Sanctification.' It is the work of the Rev. Walter Marshall, published in 1692, 'The Gospel Mystery of Sanctification.' It has at all times received the highest praise from men of eminence, both as theologians and as saints."[1]

Although Marshall's one book is short,[2] yet it is a masterpiece on sanctification and the way that holiness is related to justification and to union with Christ. Marshall was very careful in his book in arguing against the two serious errors of legalism and Antinomianism. He was shown that the power of holiness is found in Christ and not in himself. Subsequently, he wrote *The Gospel Mystery of Sanctification* gleaning the title from Paul's statement in 1 Tim 3:16: "Great is the mystery of godliness."[3] The main theme of the book is sanctification or holiness of life. For Marshall, this holiness of life consists chiefly in love to God, that is, "We must love Him

---

1. Murray, "Introduction," 1.
2. Whyte, "Appreciation of Walter Marshall," 226.
3. Beeke and Pederson, *Meet the Puritans*, 415.

as to yield ourselves wholly up to His constant service in all things, and to His disposal of us as our absolute Lord, whether it is for prosperity or adversity, life or death. And, for His sake, we are to love our neighbor—even all men, whether they are friends or foes to us."[4] This spiritual universal obedience is the great end to the attainment of which Marshall is directing the reader in his book. However, this book also deals with justification. In Marshall's view, sanctification and justification are inseparable. Therefore, we will find that the doctrine of justification is pervasive throughout the whole book. We can say that understanding Marshall's view of justification is indispensable for understanding his doctrine of sanctification. Accordingly, to understand Marshall's view on the true life of holiness, we will start with his teaching on justification. Happily, appended to Marshall's book is a sermon also entitled "The Doctrine of Justification Explained and Applied" which is a great asset in understanding Marshall's doctrine of justification in addition to his reference to the same doctrine throughout his book.

Justification

For Marshall, justification is "the means by which we are reconciled to God or having favor with God, which is described in Scripture either by forgiving our sins or by the imputation of righteousness to us (Rom 4: 5–7); because both are contained in one and the same justifying act."[5] Marshall sees justification as "the first benefit that we receive by union with Christ and the foundation of all other benefits."[6] Clearly, Marshall believes that justification is one of the benefits that we get due to union with Christ beside other benefits like sanctification and glorification. However, he is careful in distinguishing the difference between these benefits. "Justification signifies 'making just' as sanctification is 'making holy,' glorification 'making glorious.'"[7] Marshall is also careful in defining what he means by justification as "making just" so that he may remove any ambiguity. Against the Papists, he holds to the Protestant meaning of justification.

---

4. Marshall, *Gospel Mystery of Sanctification*, 2–3.
5. Marshall, *Gospel Mystery of Sanctification*, 21–22.
6. Marshall, "Doctrine of Justification Opened," 2.
7. Marshall, "Doctrine of Justification Opened," 2.

Justification Is Judicial

For Marshall, justification is a judicial term. He argues that "'making just' is not by infusion of grace and holiness into a person as the Papists teach, confounding justification and sanctification together, but 'making just' in trial and judgment, by a radical sentence discharging guilt, freeing from blame and accusation—approving, judging, owning and pronouncing a person to be righteous."[8] Then Marshall brings many proofs from the Old Testament and the New Testament to show that justification is a juridical term that has reference to trial and judgment, which is opposed to the accusation and to passing a sentence of condemnation.[9] For Marshall a person is justified when his righteousness appears when he is brought to trial. Therefore, to say that a person is made righteous would mean that his righteousness is declared. To support his argument, Marshall applies this idea to God himself "who is said to be justified when we judge of His actions as we ought to do and deem them to be righteous (Job. 32:2; Ps. 51:4; Luke 7:29)."[10] Clearly, we cannot add to the infinite righteous of God; therefore to justify God would necessarily mean to declare his righteousness. Consequently, Marshall concludes that "justification is not a real change of a sinner in himself (though a real change is annexed to it) but only a relative change with reference to God's judgment."[11]

Justification in Rom 3:23-26

Marshall takes the text in Rom 3:23–26 to explain the doctrine of justification. He uses the tool of Aristotelian causality to explain the necessity of justification. Aristotle held that "why" questions have four kinds of answers and these four kinds are named causes. The first cause is the material cause, which is the matter used. The second cause is the formal cause, which gives the matter its particular quality. The third cause is the efficient cause, which is the agent that causes the change. The fourth cause is the end or final cause, which is the sake for which the thing is done. This Aristotelian fourfold causality tool was part of the theology of the day in sixteenth- and seventeenth-century theology and had been used by the Council of Trent

---

8. Marshall, "Doctrine of Justification Opened," 2–3.
9. Marshall, "Doctrine of Justification Opened," 3.
10. Marshall, "Doctrine of Justification Opened," 4.
11. Marshall, "Doctrine of Justification Opened," 4.

(1546) to explain justification as well as by the Reformers too who responded in kind with the same distinctions.[12]

The fourfold Aristotelian causal schema was familiar to Calvin from medieval theologians.[13] Calvin used the same tool, but he was "not off upon a blind flight of philosophical fancy but demonstrated the fourfold causality from Scripture."[14] Before Marshall, Calvin used this Aristotelian tool to explain the same text in Rom 3:23–26. According to Calvin, justification has "God's mercy as the efficient cause, Christ with his blood as the meritorious cause, the formal or instrumental cause is faith in the word, and, moreover, the final cause is the glory of the divine justice and goodness."[15] In the original Aristotle scheme, the instrumental cause was not seen as a cause but as a kind of means or tool for carrying out the plan.[16] Calvin confuses the formal and the instrumental causes because in Calvin's theology the formal cause would be the plan of redemption.[17] Marshall follows Calvin in using the causal language on the same passage. Through the following eight points, Marshall explains the nature of justification:

1. The persons justified: (i) Sinners; (ii) Such sinners of all sorts that shall believe, whether Jews or gentiles.
2. The justifier, or efficient cause: God.
3. The impulsive cause: grace.
4. The means effecting, or material cause: the redemption of Christ.
5. The formal cause: the remission of sins.
6. The instrumental cause: faith.
7. The time of declaring: the present time.
8. The end: that God may appear just.

Obviously, Marshall agrees with Calvin on the efficient, material, and end causes. Unlike Calvin, he distinguishes between the formal cause and the instrumental cause. Moreover, Marshall coined a new cause which is the "impulsive cause" referring to grace. In addition to these six causes,

12. Fesko, *Beyond Calvin*, 46.
13. Helm, *John Calvin's Ideas*, 400.
14. Fesko, *Beyond Calvin*, 36–37.
15. Calvin, *Calvin's Commentaries*, Rom 3:24.
16. Helm, *John Calvin's Ideas*, 401.
17. Helm, *John Calvin's Ideas*, 401.

Marshall adds two points: (1) the persons justified and (2) the time of the declaration. Following these eight points will help us to understand Marshall's doctrine of justification.

Sinners: The Persons Justified

First of all, Marshall identifies the persons justified as sinners. He asserts two main points here. First, Marshall explains what he means by sinners. They are those who "come short of the glory of God, that is of God's approbation; of God's image of holiness; of eternal happiness."[18] Marshall emphasizes the total inability of the persons justified and of their hopeless case unless free grace restores them. The second point is the universality of this method of justification. Although the Jews are condemned by the written law and the gentiles are condemned by the light and law of nature, yet both Jews and gentiles cannot be justified except through the righteousness of God with no difference.[19] In this way, Marshall asserts that the only means to obtain the righteousness of God is by faith, and "the Jews and Gentiles are alike capable of it."[20] He also asserts that no preparation is needed from man's side that would make him suitable to be justified. Marshall elaborates on this idea of preparation in his book. In direction six he asserts that no holiness is needed as the condition whereby a person is to procure for himself a right and title to salvation.[21] In direction seven he asserts that no holiness is needed as a preparation for believing in Christ.[22] Both Jews and gentiles are problematic in this regard; and only free righteousness must be granted that can only be received by faith.

God: The Justifier or Efficient Cause

The efficient cause of justification is God. Marshall emphasizes the sovereignty of God in justification "who can justify authoritatively and irreversibly."[23] For Marshall, since God is the lawgiver, then the whole case

---

18. Marshall, "Doctrine of Justification Opened," 6.
19. Marshall, "Doctrine of Justification Opened," 6–7.
20. Marshall, "Doctrine of Justification Opened," 7.
21. Marshall, *Sanctification*, 36.
22. Marshall, *Sanctification*, 38.
23. Marshall, "Doctrine of Justification Opened," 8.

of human beings "can only be tried at His tribunal."[24] God is not merely a judge who is judging according to a law outside of himself. Our sins are against him. The debt of suffering for sin and of acting righteously is owed to him. Therefore, "God alone has the power to forgive and release the debtor."[25] For Marshall, justification is an act of God, not of men, and it flows from him.

Grace: The Impulsive Cause

The third cause that Marshall highlights is the impulsive cause of justification which is God's grace. Aristotle did not develop this cause and it does not exist in Calvin's writings. However, that grace as an impulsive cause is used later among the Puritans who were contemporaries of Marshall. For instance, Anthony Burgess (1600–1663)[26] and John Flavel (1627–91)[27] did not differentiate between the efficient cause and the impulsive cause; they saw them as one, both referring to God's grace. In another place, Flavel asserts that in the justification of a sinner, "there must be free grace for an impulsive cause."[28] Thomas Brooks (1608–80), while talking about the several springs from which the covenant of grace flows, argues that "the gracious purpose of God is the impulsive cause of our vocation, justification, glorification; it is the highest link in the golden chain of salvation."[29] The language of causation was commonly present in John Owen's (1616–83) writings. In his commentary to the Hebrews, Owen refers to God's grace as the moving and impulsive cause of the death of Christ.[30] Also Thomas Manton (1620–77), in his sermon on Titus 2:11–14 argues that "the impulsive cause of election is God's grace,"[31] since grace is the first moving cause of all the blessings that we have from God.

The emphasis on grace as an impulsive cause for justification was important for Marshall to confront any notion of human works or merits in justification. Marshall points out that the emphasis on the freeness of God's

24. Marshall, "Doctrine of Justification Opened," 8.
25. Marshall, "Doctrine of Justification Opened," 8.
26. Burgess, *True Doctrine of Justification*, 2.
27. Flavel, *Fountain of Life Opened*, 136.
28. Flavel, *Method of Grace*, 136.
29. Brooks, *Works of Thomas Brooks*, 316–17.
30. Owen, *Exposition of the Epistle to the Hebrews*, 160.
31. Manton, *Complete Works of Thomas Manton*, 39.

grace "signifies God's free undeserved favor, in opposition to any works of our own righteousness whereby it might be challenged as a debt to us."[32] He shows that the impulsive cause cannot be according to our works for two reasons. First, "there was not, nor is anything in us, but what might move God to condemn us, for we have all sinned."[33] Second, "God would take away boasting and have His grace glorified and exalted in our salvation."[34]

Marshall confronted those who try to argue that the doctrine of justification out of free grace would lead to Antinomianism. In expressing their position, Marshall says: "They have persuaded themselves that such a way of justification is ineffectual, yea, destructive to sanctification, and that the practice of sincere obedience cannot be established against Antinomian dotages and prevailing lusts, except it is made the necessary condition of our justification, and so of our eternal salvation."[35] He views their position as subtle, because although they distinguish between the law and the gospel in their words, yet they still embrace a legalist position.

Marshall's adversaries argued that "the law requires to do all its commandments perfectly that we may live, whereas because of grace we have a milder condition now which is sincere doing, that we may live."[36] These adversaries would defend their position saying that both salvation and the sincere obedience needed are given to them freely by the grace of Christ.[37] However, Marshall refuses any notion of works as a condition for justification. He describes their position as "a fallacious wizard on a legal way of salvation, to make it look like pure gospel."[38] In Marshall's view, "the difference between the law and gospel does not at all consist in this, that the one requires perfect doing; the other, only sincere doing; but in this, that the one requires doing; the other, not doing, but believing for life and salvation. Their terms are different, not only in degree, but in their whole nature."[39]

Therefore, for Marshall, no middle way can exist between justification by law and justification by grace alone. Neither perfect obedience nor sincere obedience can ever lead to justification. Any attempt to be justified by

---

32. Marshall, "Doctrine of Justification Opened," 8.
33. Marshall, "Doctrine of Justification Opened," 9.
34. Marshall, "Doctrine of Justification Opened," 9.
35. Marshall, *Gospel Mystery of Sanctification*, 100.
36. Marshall, *Gospel Mystery of Sanctification*, 101.
37. Marshall, *Gospel Mystery of Sanctification*, 101.
38. Marshall, *Gospel Mystery of Sanctification*, 102.
39. Marshall, *Gospel Mystery of Sanctification*, 105.

the law, even by sincere obedience if not perfect obedience, is condemned. The reason is that this attempt puts the person automatically under the obligation of fulfilling the whole law.[40] "But we are saved by grace, as the immediate and complete cause of our whole salvation, excluding procurement of our salvation by the condition of works and claiming it by any law as a due debt."[41]

Marshall also refutes another subtle technique that would ground salvation on works rather than on free grace. In direction six of his book, he opposes any reference to our works that would make them the procuring conditions and cases of our salvation by Christ. In direction seven, Marshall refuses the idea that makes works "necessary preparatives to fit us for receiving Christ and His salvation by faith."[42] According to Marshall, those who hold to the preparation idea argue that preparing ourselves to receive a free gift does not contradict the freeness of grace.[43] Marshall also sees this doctrine as being in opposition to God's grace and as being a return to "those legal terms of doing first the duties required in the law, that so we may live."[44] The inevitable result for trying to prepare ourselves for receiving grace is frustration.

For Marshall, "to try to make ourselves fit for Christ is to be led away from Christ by a satanic delusion."[45] The real need is to receive Christ who justifies the ungodly, by faith. We are not required to be godly before we believe.[46] Rather, "what people really need is union with Christ."[47] Therefore, Marshall turns now to the material cause of our justification, which is the redemption of Christ.

Redemption of Christ: Material Cause

The next cause for justification is the material cause or the effecting means as Marshall calls it.[48] Marshall uses the two words in Rom 3:23–26 that are

40. Marshall, *Gospel Mystery of Sanctification*, 105.
41. Marshall, *Gospel Mystery of Sanctification*, 111.
42. Marshall, *Gospel Mystery of Sanctification*, 130.
43. Marshall, *Gospel Mystery of Sanctification*, 130.
44. Marshall, *Gospel Mystery of Sanctification*, 131.
45. Beeke, "Introduction," xiii.
46. Marshall, *Gospel Mystery of Sanctification*, 133.
47. Beeke, "Introduction," xiii.
48. Marshall, "Doctrine of Justification Opened," 9.

related to Christ's death, "redemption" and "propitiation," to explain how the work of Christ relates to justification. For Marshall, the word "redemption" refers to deliverance made by paying a price, which is Christ's death. Christ's death "was the price of our redemption, that we might be justified in God's sight."[49] However, Marshall does not see Christ's redemption in his death only. He argues that Christ's suffering "was the consummating act of redemption, and so all is attributed to it (Heb 2:9,10)—even to His blood, though other doings and sufferings concur (2 Cor 8: 9)."[50]

The other word that is related to Christ's death here is "propitiation." For Marshall, this word is a double-sided coin. In propitiation, God's wrath is appeased on one hand, and on the other hand, his favor is won. Marshall used two pictures from the Old Testament to describe this double meaning of "propitiation": The first one is the propitiatory sacrifices whose blood was shed to appease God's wrath. The second is "the mercy seat which was called propitiation, because it covered the ark wherein was the law, and the blood of the sacrifices for atonement was sprinkled by the high priest before it. And this mercy seat was a sign of God's favorableness to a sinful people in residing among them."[51] Calvin understands justification similarly as a gracious acceptance by God and as forgiveness of sins.[52]

These two aspects in Christ's work by which God's wrath is removed and His favor is guaranteed are central to Marshall's view of justification. The necessary consequence of these two aspects in justification is that we are reconciled with God. Marshall argues that this reconciliation is "described in Scripture, either by forgiving our sins, or by the imputation of righteousness to us (Rom. 4:5–7); because both are contained in one and the same justifying act." He understands that justification contains not only a negative aspect in which sins are forgiven but also a positive aspect is also essential to justification, which is the imputation of the righteousness of Christ. He says, "We are justified by a righteousness wrought out in Christ and imputed to us."[53] Therefore, God's acceptance of us is not only related to the remission of our sins but also related to the imputation of Christ's righteousness by which we win God's favor.

---

49. Marshall, "Doctrine of Justification Opened," 10.
50. Marshall, "Doctrine of Justification Opened," 11.
51. Marshall, "Doctrine of Justification Opened," 10.
52. Calvin, *Inst.* 3.11.4.
53. Marshall, *Gospel Mystery of Sanctification*, 41.

This forgiveness of sin and imputation of righteousness is related not only to Christ's death but also to his active obedience. Marshall says, "The righteousness that Christ wrought for us by His obedience to death is imputed to us for our justification."[54] For Marshall, what was imputed for us as righteousness was not only Christ's obedience in his death but also Christ's obedience in his life to the law. Actually, Marshall uses the terms "passive" and "active" obedience of Christ as both related to our justification. He argues that

> He [Christ] subjected Himself to the law, in active as well as passive obedience (Gal 4:4) and obeyed His Father even to death, doing and suffering at His commandment (John 14:31; Heb 10:7), and His obedience for our justification. Compare Romans 5:19 with Philippians 3:8,9. So Christ satisfied both our debt of righteousness and debt of punishment, for our faultiness, taint of sin and want of righteousness, as well as for our guilt and obnoxiousness to punishment, that we might be free from wrath and deemed righteous in God's sight.[55]

Marshall was aware that making the imputed righteousness of Christ and his active obedience as essential to justification provokes some fears. Those who were against Antinomianism argued that "this doctrine tends to the subversion of a holy practice, and is a great pillar of Antinomianism."[56] Yet Marshall did not sacrifice the imputation of Christ's righteousness in our justification on the altar of fear for Antinomianism. Actually, Marshall will argue in his book that without this doctrine there cannot be any holiness, as we will see later.

This concern regarding the imputation of Christ's righteousness and his active obedience for our justification was not new. Similar fears existed in the Westminster Assembly as we have seen before. Although the main view in the assembly was that Christ's active obedience was imputed for justification, divines like Thomas Gataker (1577–1654) and Richard Vines (1599–1656) rejected the idea of the imputation of Christ's obedience for justification.[57] Their greatest concern was to avoid any hint of Antinomi-

---

54. Marshall, *Gospel Mystery of Sanctification*, 56.
55. Marshall, "Doctrine of Justification Opened," 11.
56. Marshall, *Gospel Mystery of Sanctification*, 22.
57. Letham, *Westminster Assembly*, 253.

anism, since including the active obedience of Christ in our justification would nullify the need for personal holiness.[58]

Similar to Walter Marshall's view, many divines argued for the imputation of the active obedience of Christ, such as Joshua Hoyle (d. 1654), Thomas Goodwin (1600–1680), Lazarus Seaman (d. 1675), William Gouge (1575–1653), Daniel Featley (1582–1645) and George Walker (c. 1581–1651).[59] Actually Goodwin, who definitely knew Marshall and consulted with him during Marshall's spiritual anxieties,[60] presented many arguments for the necessity of the imputation of Christ's active obedience for justification. The final wording of article 11 about justification in the *Westminster Confession of Faith* is "obedience and satisfaction of Christ" which can be seen as an accommodation to the opponents of the imputation of the active obedience of Christ.[61] However, a holistic view of the Westminster Standards shows that the divines continued to believe in the imputation of Christ's active obedience for justification.[62] Moreover, the *Savoy Declaration* (1658) which was a modified statement of the *Westminster Confession* under the supervision of Goodwin and John Owen (1616–83),[63] clearly held to the imputation of the active obedience of Christ.[64] Therefore, in spite of the fear of Antinomianism, Marshall follows the Reformed teaching of the Westminster Assembly and *Savoy Declaration* and emphasized the active obedience of Christ for justification.

In sum, Marshall stresses the centrality of Christ and his work as the material cause for justification. He frames his understanding of Christ's centrality in justification through three main points: The death of Christ, the resurrection of Christ, and union with Christ. First, Christ obeyed and died to be our ransom so that we might be justified in God's sight.[65] Second, "God accepted this price as a satisfaction to His justice, which He showed in raising Christ from the dead and so accepting Him for all our sins."[66]

---

58. Letham, *Westminster Assembly*, 263.
59. Fesko, *Theology of the Westminster Standards*, 214.
60. McRae, "Introduction," 10–11.
61. Fesko, *Theology of the Westminster Standards*, 217.
62. Fesko, *Theology of the Westminster Standards*, 224.
63. Fesko, *Theology of the Westminster Standards*, 224.
64. *Savoy Declaration*, chapter 11.
65. Marshall, "Doctrine of Justification Opened," 11.
66. Marshall, "Doctrine of Justification Opened," 11.

Third, "this redemption is in Christ, as to the benefit of it, so that it cannot be had except we be in Christ and have Christ."[67]

Remission of Sins: Formal Cause

Unlike Calvin, Marshall distinguishes between the formal and the instrumental causes. For Marshall, the formal cause is the remission of sins, which is strongly connected to the previous cause; the material cause. According to Marshall, "The formal cause of justification, or that wherein it consists, is the remission of sin, that is, not only the guilt and punishment is removed, but the fault; because it is a pardon grounded on justice, which clears the fault also."[68] This cause may be confusing for some because Marshall seemingly argues that the formal cause of justification only concerns the forgiveness of sins. Furthermore, this explanation may cause some to think that Marshall does not think that the imputation of Christ's righteousness is included in justification.

However, this interpretation of Marshall's formal cause would contradict what we have just been saying about his explanation of the material cause. Moreover, Marshall himself goes on to explain what he means by the remission of sins as a formal cause of justification. For him, not imputing sin, that is remission of sins, and imputing righteousness are inseparable and both happen through the bloodshed of Christ. He argues, "In men, subject to a law, there is no middle condition between not imputing sin and imputing righteousness, and so these terms are used as equivalent."[69] But the question remains, why did Marshall choose to express the formal cause as remission of sins only in his sermon? A possible answer is that he wanted to tie together all the causes to the language used in Rom 3:23–26.

Up to this point, we see how Marshall's ideas are coherent and systematized: We are sinners. God is the one who can forgive and reconcile us to himself out of mere mercy and grace. This reconciliation happens through the redeeming work of Christ. The redemption of Christ can only benefit us if we are united to him (1 Cor 1:30). This flow of ideas raises the question: How can this redemption be related to us? How can Christ's work that is gracious be received by us and become ours? These questions lead us to the instrumental cause of justification.

67. Marshall, "Doctrine of Justification Opened," 12.
68. Marshall, "Doctrine of Justification Opened," 12.
69. Marshall, "Doctrine of Justification Opened," 12.

Faith: Instrumental Cause

Like Calvin,[70] Marshall argues that faith is the instrumental cause for justification, which is the Protestant position in general.[71] In simpler words, for Marshall, "faith is the means and instrument by which we receive Christ and all His fullness actually in our hearts."[72] The relation between faith and justification was debatable. Therefore, the use of the word "instrument" in reference to faith in the Reformed tradition was widely used, such as in the *Belgic Confession of Faith* (1561, article 22) and the *Westminster Confession of Faith* (1647, chapter 11.2).[73] The word "instrument" is intended to avoid any misconception of the meaning of faith in relation to justification. Marshall follows the same pattern of the Reformed tradition, and he explains in his sermon and his book what this instrumental use of faith means. He asserts several points in his explanation.

First, Marshall argues that justification by faith in Christ is antithetical to justification by works.[74] He believes that men are unable to obtain justification by works. "Our natural state has the property never to be good."[75] Then, if we seek salvation on condition of works, "we bring ourselves under the terms of the law and become debtors to fulfil the whole law in perfection,"[76] a scenario which can never happen. On the other hand, justification by faith means that we are justified not by doing but by believing. "We believe in Christ for justification out of a sense of our inability to obtain justification by works."[77] For Marshall, "faith that is required for our salvation in the gospel is to be understood in a sense contrary to doing works as a condition to procure our salvation."[78] He emphasizes the dichotomy between the terms the law and the gospel.

Second, Marshall is keen to assert that faith itself is not a work, by which we earn justification. He does not oppose the idea that faith is required for our salvation. However, he opposed the Arminian doctrine of

---

70. Calvin, *Calvin's Commentaries*, Rom 3:24.
71. Beeke, "Relation of Faith to Justification," 89.
72. Marshall, *Gospel Mystery of Sanctification*, 64.
73. Beeke, "Relation of Faith to Justification," 60.
74. Marshall, "Doctrine of Justification Opened," 13.
75. Marshall, *Gospel Mystery of Sanctification*, 88.
76. Marshall, *Gospel Mystery of Sanctification*, 105.
77. Marshall, "Doctrine of Justification Opened," 13.
78. Marshall, *Gospel Mystery of Sanctification*, 111.

justification by faith. Arminianism advocates conditional faith unto justification.[79] For Arminius, faith is foundational for justification and not instrumental.[80] But Marshall teaches that the requirement of faith is to be understood "in a sense contrary to doing good works as a condition to procure our salvation."[81] Marshall asserts that considering faith as an act of righteousness that earns our justification would have been justification by works.[82]

Furthermore, Marshall argues that if we consider faith as an act of righteousness to procure justification, then justification is not of free grace. Faith must be an instrumental cause, otherwise the whole argument of grace as an impulsive cause of justification is nullified. He says

> Christ, with all His salvation, is freely given by the grace of God to all that believe on Him, for we are saved by grace through faith.... Now, that which is a gift of grace must not at all be earned, purchased or procured by any work, or works performed as a condition to get a right or title to it. Therefore, faith itself must not be accounted such a conditional work. If it is by grace, it is no more of works; otherwise grace is no more grace (Rom. 11:6). The condition of a free gift is only take, and have. And in this sense we will readily acknowledge faith to be a condition, allowing a liberty in terms where we agree in the thing.[83]

Marshall uses the word "condition" in relation to faith with reservation. The reason for this reservation is that "faith cannot be a condition to procure a mere right or title to Christ."[84] Therefore, Marshall prefers the word "instrument": "For a condition generally denotes a meritorious quality for the sake of which a benefit is conferred."[85] He asserts the instrumentally of faith rather than conditionality by the illustration of a peppercorn in both his book,[86] and in his sermon.[87] Marshall opposes those who consider faith as small as a peppercorn if compared to the gift of Christ. Yet they believe

---

79. Beeke, "Relation of Faith to Justification," 91.
80. Arminius, *Works of James Arminius*, 2:50n.
81. Marshall, *Gospel Mystery of Sanctification*, 111.
82. Marshall, "Doctrine of Justification Opened," 13.
83. Marshall, *Gospel Mystery of Sanctification*, 68–69.
84. Marshall, *Gospel Mystery of Sanctification*, 68.
85. Beeke, "Relation of Faith to Justification," 62.
86. Marshall, *Gospel Mystery of Sanctification*, 69.
87. Marshall, "Doctrine of Justification Opened," 13.

that this peppercorn is the payment needed to be justified. He replies, "If you give a peppercorn to purchase a title to it, then you spoil the freeness of the gift."[88] To summarize Marshall's view of how faith is an instrument and not a condition, the following lines can be of great help:

> Therefore, we must not here consider faith as a work of righteousness performed or done, as a condition to procure right and title to Christ, as the hand by which we work to earn Him as our bread and drink, as our wages; but only as the hand by which we receive Christ, as freely given to us or as the mouth by which we eat and drink Him.[89]

Errors that relate to faith and its relation to justification were present in both Neonomianism and Antinomianism. While Neonomianism views faith as some kind of virtue by which we procure justification, Antinomianism, in reaction, wants to avoid any hint of contribution from man's side in his justification. Accordingly, Antinomianism teaches that faith is only a manifestation of justification which had already happened in eternity.[90] The Westminster Assembly faced both errors by clarifying the instrumental role of faith in our justification in the *Confession* (11.1), the *Larger Catechism* (Q 70) and the *Shorter Catechism* (Q 33). In his book, Marshall only confronted one of these two errors regarding the role of faith in justification, which is the legalistic error. He does not refer to the danger of eternal justification in his book as a fear for Antinomianism, which shows that he is more concerned with legalism or Neonomianism.

The third point that Marshall asserts in his explanation of the role of faith is the object to which faith points. For Marshall, what justifies us is not faith itself but Christ and his righteousness. Faith is the instrument by which we receive Christ and his righteousness and thus are justified. In order to explain his idea, Marshall uses the illustration of eating and drinking. He says,

> The Scripture illustrates this receiving by the similitude of eating and drinking: He that believes on Christ drinks the living water of His Spirit (John 7:37–39). Christ is the bread of life; His flesh is meat indeed, and His blood is drink indeed. And the way to eat and drink it is to believe in Christ and, by so doing, we dwell in Christ, and Christ in us, and we have everlasting life (John 6:35,

---

88. Marshall, *Gospel Mystery of Sanctification*, 69.
89. Marshall, *Gospel Mystery of Sanctification*, 112.
90. Van Dixhoorn, "Strange Silence of Prolocutor Twisse," 405–6.

47, 48, 54–56). How can it be taught more clearly that we receive Christ Himself properly into our souls by faith, as we receive food into our bodies by eating and drinking, and that Christ is as truly united to us in this way as our food when we eat or drink it?[91]

Marshall does not deny that the Scripture says that we are justified by faith. However, he explains this expression to mean that we are justified by Christ whom we receive by faith. Marshall expresses his idea by saying, "We are justified by faith only metonymically,[92] by reason of the righteousness received by it; and to be "justified by faith" and "by Christ" is all one (Gal. 3:8; Rom. 5:19)."[93] In his sermon he also uses the eating and drinking illustrations to argue for that meaning. Marshall says, "As a man may be said to be maintained by his hands, or nourished by his mouth, when those do but receive that which nourishes—his food and drink. The cup is put for the liquor in the cup."[94]

To conclude, Marshall believes that faith is the instrument by which "we have the actual enjoyment and possession of Christ Himself";[95] we do not only have "remission of sin, but also we receive the gift of righteousness."[96]

The Present Time: Time of Declaration

Marshall argues that we are justified by God's righteousness. This justification can be true because "God in setting forth Christ to be a propitiation through faith in His blood aimed to declare His righteousness now under the gospel."[97] Marshall asserts two points regarding the time of declaration. First, God's righteousness is what is declared. In this point, Marshall explains that the meaning of God's righteousness here is not "the essential righteousness, that which is an essential property of God, but righteousness, which is upon all them that believe—Christ's righteousness, which is the end of the law (Rom 10:3, 4), and therefore called 'God's righteousness,'

---

91. Marshall, *Gospel Mystery of Sanctification*, 68.
92. Metonymy is a figure of speech in which a thing or concept is called not by its own name but rather by a metonym, the name of something associated in meaning with that thing or concept.
93. Marshall, "Doctrine of Justification Opened," 13.
94. Marshall, "Doctrine of Justification Opened," 13–14.
95. Marshall, *Gospel Mystery of Sanctification*, 67.
96. Marshall, "Doctrine of Justification Opened," 15.
97. Marshall, "Doctrine of Justification Opened," 14.

that which Christ wrought for us, which is given to us and we receive by faith; that by which Christ answered the law for us, by which as the price, He redeemed us."[98]

Second, God's forgiveness, whether in the Old Testament or the New Testament, was based on Christ's atonement. Even though the same righteousness of Christ was the basis for pardoning sins both in the Old Testament and in the New Testament, this righteousness was not declared clearly until the gospel times. Marshall argues that in the Old Testament this righteousness was only "shadowed out by the sacrifices, ransoms, redemptions, etc."[99] Therefore, during the times of the Old Testament, God pardoned sins without present satisfaction. According to Marshall, "God had patience and did not exact the debt, until Christ paid all."[100] God's righteousness was revealed by the coming of Christ.

God's Justice: End Cause

Marshall concludes his explanation of justification by the end cause, which is the manifestation of God's justice. The end cause of justification is that God may appear just in forgiving sins past as well as present. For if God forgives sins without satisfaction, he is unjust. But through the death of Christ we are justified, and the justice of God is revealed. For Marshall, God's justice and mercy meet in our salvation.[101] Moreover, through Christ's work, God is revealed to be the only procurer and worker of our righteousness and so our justifier, so that we may glory in God only.[102] This is the end cause for Marshall, that is to glorify God's name.

Conclusion

To conclude, Marshall holds to the Protestant doctrine of justification which can be expressed by the expression "Justification by Faith Alone." These four words express most of Marshall's belief of justification. For him "justification" is a judicial term that relates to our reconciliation as sinners

---

98. Marshall, "Doctrine of Justification Opened," 15.
99. Marshall, "Doctrine of Justification Opened," 16.
100. Marshall, "Doctrine of Justification Opened," 16.
101. Marshall, "Doctrine of Justification Opened," 17.
102. Marshall, "Doctrine of Justification Opened," 17.

with the holy God. It is described in Scripture either by forgiving our sins or by the imputation of righteousness to us. The preposition "by" teaches that we are justified by the instrumentality of faith, by which we receive Christ and all his benefits. The word "faith" means to trust in Jesus Christ. Marshall follows the Reformed belief of faith as "casting all our cares on Christ."[103] Marshall does not count justifying faith as work of merit. "Although faith is an act, it is not a work of merit."[104] The object of faith is Christ. Marshall believes that Christ is the object of our faith by whom we are justified.

Finally, the word "alone" denotes the freeness of God's grace in justification. This word "alone" defines "the difference between biblical Christianity and all its counterfeits." For Marshall, we cannot add anything to God's accomplishment in our salvation. The only reason for one to be saved lies in God alone and his mercy. As Marshall teaches, God's grace is the impulsive cause for our justification. If anyone is saved, then he is saved by Christ alone. Accordingly, "God saves us by faith, that all the glory may be ascribed to His free grace."[105]

For Marshall, the doctrine of justification was not a theoretical called doctrine that only stays in the books but a doctrine that touches the hearts and changes the lives. Therefore, he ends his sermon on justification by some practical applications of that doctrine.

Encouragement and Consolation

Marshall argues that being justified means that we are delivered from the charge of sin and fault before God. This deliverance causes "great happiness as our sins are forgiven and we are accounted just in the sight of the judge of the world."[106] For Marshall, reconciliation with God is the greatest blessing we can ever have. He says, "The wrath of God is an unsupportable burden and the foundation of all miseries, which foundation is razed and a foundation of blessedness laid, by which we have peace with God and are fully reconciled to God."[107]

Moreover, consolation includes freedom from the burden of seeking salvation by the works of the law. Marshall uses biblical terms that

103. Gerstner, "Nature of Justifying Faith," 107.
104. Gerstner, "Nature of Justifying Faith," 108.
105. Marshall, *Gospel Mystery of Sanctification*, 77.
106. Marshall, "Doctrine of Justification Opened," 17.
107. Marshall, "Doctrine of Justification Opened," 18.

are attached to the law which show how fearful is living under the law: wrath-working law (Rom 4:15); from a sin-irritating law (Rom 6:5); from a killing law, a ministration of death and condemnation (2 Cor 3:6, 7, 9).[108] Consequently, the justified are "delivered from a condemning conscience which otherwise would still gnaw them as a worm"[109]

Another point of consolation is the eternality of Christ's righteousness. For Marshall, Christ's righteousness is everlasting by which our standing with Christ is secured. That righteousness which is "more powerful to save than Adam's sin was to destroy or condemn."[110] Furthermore, Marshall teaches that justification changes our attitude towards God's justice. God's justice is dreadful to natural people. This justice provided "a divine mandate to condemn them, and therefore they hate it, as was case with Martin Luther."[111] According to Marshall, God's justice to believers is converted from being something to fear to being something that we would appeal to because of the mercy granted to us in Christ.[112]

Finally, justification for Marshall is a consolation in troubles and suffering. For the justified, "all things shall work for good through grace to bring them to glory, because God is for them, who is the Creator and Governor of all things."[113]

Are We in Christ?

The second use of the doctrine of justification is examining whether we are in Christ or not. According to Marshall, we examine different things in the light of justification. For instance, "we consider whether we became sensible of sin and our condemnation or not. Without a sense of sin, there will be no prizing of Christ or desire to holiness."[114] Do we rely on anything within ourselves for justification, or "do we only trust on free mercy for justification in God's sight?"[115] Do we have enough confidence in Christ? Marshall understands that "sometimes believing souls may be attacked by

---

108. Marshall, "Doctrine of Justification Opened," 19.
109. Marshall, "Doctrine of Justification Opened," 19.
110. Marshall, "Doctrine of Justification Opened," 20.
111. Beeke, "Relation of Faith to Justification," 53.
112. Marshall, "Doctrine of Justification Opened," 20–21.
113. Marshall, "Doctrine of Justification Opened," 21.
114. Marshall, "Doctrine of Justification Opened," 22.
115. Marshall, "Doctrine of Justification Opened," 23.

doubts, yet it fights against them and never gives up to the dominion of them."[116] Do we walk in holiness as an evidence that our faith is alive and not dead?

Exhortations to Several Duties

Marshall classifies people under three categories: sinners who do not care about being justified; other people who are also sinners but want to be justified through their works; and those who are justified. In this way, Marshall includes all human beings, and he showed that the doctrine of justification is important for the three groups.

For the wicked, this doctrine can be a warning from going further in sin and about the severity of God's wrath. Justification is a great door of mercy.[117] For those who have a mind to turn to God through their works, Marshall encourages them to quit this way: Trying to be justified through our works will make us "weary for very vanity and be under continuous discomfort and discouragement."[118] Finally, Marshall exhorts the justified by faith to walk humbly, to praise and glorify God, to walk comfortably, to hold fast to this way of justification in spite of all attacks, and to walk as one that enjoys the favor of God in Christ and therefore, to walk in holiness.[119]

Obviously, Marshall makes a strong connection between justification and holiness of life. His doctrine of justification will be essential in his understanding of sanctification and the way that sanctification and justification relate to each other. In the next chapters, we will investigate Marshall's teaching of sanctification and how justification and sanctification relate to each other.

---

116. Marshall, "Doctrine of Justification Opened," 23.
117. Marshall, "Doctrine of Justification Opened," 25.
118. Marshall, "Doctrine of Justification Opened," 27.
119. Marshall, "Doctrine of Justification Opened," 28–30.

CHAPTER 4

Marshall on Sanctification

According to the *Westminster Shorter Catechism* (question 35), sanctification is "the work of God's free grace whereby we are renewed in the whole man after the image of God, and are enabled more and more to die unto sin, and live unto righteousness." In this definition, sanctification is defined as a lifelong process of being conformed to the image of Christ and thereby being enabled to grow in the practice of true holiness. John Owen explains sanctification briefly as "the universal renovation of our nature by the Holy Spirit into the image of God, through Jesus Christ."[1] Generally, the Reformed theology views sanctification as an inevitable "stage in the *ordo salutis*; the link between regeneration and glorification, in which sanctification is glorification begun as glorification is sanctification completed."[2] Although many books have been written on this important doctrine, Marshall's book *The Gospel Mystery of Sanctification* continues to be regarded as an eminent classic Puritan work on sanctification.[3]

Andrew Murray expressed his regret that "this book is not better known among the members of our Christian churches."[4] Marshall explains the doctrine of sanctification in a way that opposes the two errors of Antinomianism and Neonomianism. Against Antinomianism, he affirms the importance of a godly life and of holiness; however, he also argues against

---

1. Owen, *Works of John Owen*, 3:386.
2. Packer, "'Keswick' and the Reformed Doctrine," 154.
3. Beeke and Pederson, *Meet the Puritans*, 416.
4. Murray, "Introduction," 1.

Neonomianism that would make the gospel a "new law" which needs to be obeyed to achieve godliness.[5] We see a warm recommendation of this book in the preface of the Edinburgh edition of 1733 of Marshall's book, signed by "Ebenezer Erskine, the founder of the Scottish Secession Church and his brother Ralph, together with such other ministers of the Kirk and the Associate Presbytery as Alexander Hamilton, James Wardlaw, James Oglivie and James Gibb."[6] They commended it as "one of the most useful books the world hath seen for many years. Its excellence is, that it leads the serious reader directly to Jesus Christ, and cuts the sinews and overturns the foundation of the new divinity by the same argument of gospel holiness, by which many attempt to overturn the old."[7]

Although Marshall deals with justification in his book as well, justification itself is not an end in itself; rather it is means to an end, which is holiness, and this is the main subject of the book. Marshall comments on the use of the doctrine of justification in his sermon that is appended to his book and says, "Do you come to Christ for remission of sins for the right end, namely, that you may be freed from the dominion of sin before the living God (Heb 9:14; Ps 130; Titus 2:14; 1 Pet 2:24)? If otherwise, you do not receive it for the right end and do not desire really the favour and enjoyment of God and to be in friendship with Him."[8] The main aim for Marshall in his book is to answer the question: How a person can be made holy? And this aim is clarified in the title he chose for the book *The Gospel Mystery of Sanctification.*

In the current chapter, we will investigate Marshall's doctrine of sanctification. Marshall's concern is not only to give a right understanding of holiness but also to show what the right means to this holiness are. Marshall's doctrine of sanctification can be understood in the light of four main points: The definition of the true meaning of holiness, the human inability to achieve holiness, the qualifications or endowments that are needed and without which the practical life of holiness is impossible, and finally, the means by which we obtain these qualifications or endowments that enable us to be holy.

---

5. Beeke, "Introduction," viii.
6. Wood, "Walter Marshall," 23.
7. Erskine et al., "Recommendatory Preface," vi.
8. Marshall, "Doctrine of Justification Opened," 24.

Sanctification or Holiness

In his first direction,[9] Marshall starts to lay the ground for his work that aims to show how a person can perform duties of holiness and righteousness required in the law. Before showing the method of attaining godliness, Marshall gives a brief definition of holiness as the obedience which "God requires of us in the law, particularly in the moral law, summed up in the Ten Commandments, and more briefly in those two great commandments of love to God and our neighbor (Matt. 22:37, 39), and more largely, explained throughout the Holy Scriptures."[10] For Marshall, holiness means conformity to God's law, that is to obey God. However, he argues that this holiness should flow from love and delight to do the will of God and from fear. He says,

> This holiness consists not only in external works of piety and charity, but in the holy thoughts, imaginations and affections of the soul, and chiefly in love, from whence all other good works must flow, or else they are not acceptable to God; not only in refraining the execution of sinful lusts, but in longing and delighting to do the will of God and in a cheerful obedience to God, without repining, fretting, grudging at any duty, as if it were a grievous yoke and burden to you.[11]

Marshall argues that holiness is a word that finds its meaning in relation to God's law. To be holy means to obey God's law. This view of sanctification as fulfillment of the law characterized Puritan theology of sanctification.[12] On the other hand, different groups have differing views about how to relate to the law. As Cheul Lee summarizes: "The Antinomians denied the binding authority of any written law for believers. The Neonomians accepted the abolition of the Decalogue while making the commandment of Christ the new law for evangelical righteousness. The Arminians made the observation of the moral law a condition for a greater measure of grace from God."[13] Marshall follows the general Puritan view of the law. What he means by holiness is to love God as our absolute Lord

---

9. Marshall uses the word "directions" instead of "chapters" in his book.
10. Marshall, *Gospel Mystery of Sanctification*, 1.
11. Marshall, *Gospel Mystery of Sanctification*, 2.
12. Kevan, *Grace of Law*, 21.
13. Lee, "Sanctification by Faith," 69.

in every aspect of our lives and, for his sake, to love our neighbor.[14] This understanding of holiness resembles Christ's answer in Matt 22:37–40, in which fulfilling the law means to love God from all our heart, soul, and mind, and to love our neighbor as ourselves.[15]

Therefore, Marshall is clearly against Antinomianism. He asserts that "the best morally principal man is the greatest saint; and that morality is the principal part of true religion, and the test of all other parts, without which faith is dead and all other religious performances are a vain show and mere hypocrisy."[16] Marshall's approach to the place of obedience to the law in the lives of believers follows the pattern of Calvin's theology and of post-Reformation theology. The traditional trend then was to speak of the three uses of the law: "*usus politicus*, to restrain sin; *usus pedagogus*, to lead to Christ, and *usus normativus*, to determine the believer's conduct."[17]

Our concern here is the *usus normativus*, which Calvin emphasized in his writings. Calvin said, "The third and principal use, which pertains more closely to the proper purpose of the law, finds its place among believers in whose hearts the Spirit of God already lives and reigns."[18] The reformer was against any notion of abandoning the Mosaic law entirely. He added, "Certain ignorant persons, not understanding this distinction, rashly cast out the whole of Moses, and bid farewell to the two Tables of the Law."[19] Calvin viewed the abrogation of the law "as suspension of its power to bind conscience not as suspension of its commandments; it continues to demand believers of full obedience."[20] However, Calvin was aware that conformity to the law is a lifelong process that ends by the end of our life, for "the law points out the goal toward which throughout life we are to strive."[21] Marshall expresses similar ideas on the obedience to the law when he says,

> Observe that the most I promise is no more than an acceptable performance of these duties of the law such as our gracious merciful God will certainly delight in and be pleased with during our

---

14. Marshall, *Gospel Mystery of Sanctification*, 3.
15. Marshall, *Gospel Mystery of Sanctification*, 5.
16. Marshall, *Gospel Mystery of Sanctification*, 5.
17. Kevan, *Grace of Law*, 38.
18. Calvin, *Inst.* 3.7.12.
19. Calvin, *Inst.* 2.7.13.
20. Ngun, "Survey of the Role of the Law," 50.
21. Calvin, *Inst.* 2.7.13.

state of imperfection in this world, and such as will end in perfection of holiness and all happiness in the world to come.[22]

Similarly, the *Westminster Confession* follows Calvin's pattern and teaches the importance of the obedience to the law in the lives of believers. In chapter 19, "Of the Law of God," the *Westminster Confession* says: "The moral law does forever bind all, as well justified persons as others, to the obedience thereof; and that, not only in regard of the matter contained in it, but also in respect of the authority of God the creator, who gave it. Neither does Christ, in the gospel, any way dissolve, but much strengthen this obligation."[23] One of the Westminster Assembly's concerns was Antinomianism; hence the divines were keen to show the necessity of the obedience to the law of God even in the lives of the believers. Among those of the divines who wrote against Antinomianism and who emphasized the importance of obeying God's law were Thomas Gataker (1574–1654), Samuel Rutherford (1600–1661), Richard Baxter (1615–91), and Anthony Burgess (d. 1664). The Assembly highlighted the way that "Christ and his gospel actually strengthened our obligation to keep the law of God."[24] For the divines, keeping the law binds everyone, as "God forever remains the Creator who is also the law-giver and we remain His subjects."[25] Therefore, the *Confession* maintains the continuing validity of the law as a rule of life for believers.[26] This Creator-creature relationship that binds us to conform to God's law, whether we are justified or not, is resonated in Marshall's thoughts. Marshall argues that "the law is holy, just and good in its nature (Rom 7:12) and suitable for us to perform because of our natural relation to our Creator and fellow creatures."[27]

Marshall believes that holiness is the original aim for which we were first created in the image of God, that is, to love God above all and to love our neighbor for his sake. Therefore, for Marshall, sanctification is the renewal of that beautiful image in our new creation by Jesus Christ and this renewal shall be perfected in our glorification.[28] Accordingly, Marshall views the moral law as binding upon all humanity, whether in the pre-fall

22. Marshall, *Gospel Mystery of Sanctification*, 3.
23. *Westminster Confession of Faith* 19.5.
24. Van Dixhoorn, *Confessing the Faith*, 248.
25. Van Dixhoorn, *Confessing the Faith*, 247.
26. Ngun, "Survey of the Role of the Law," 60.
27. Marshall, *Gospel Mystery of Sanctification*, 4.
28. Marshall, *Gospel Mystery of Sanctification*, 3.

or the post-fall stage of redemptive history,[29] and whether a person is justified or not. To conclude, Marshall comments on the believers' relation to the moral law by saying that "we must still practice moral duties as commanded by Moses, but we must not seek to be justified by our practice. If we use them as a rule of life, not as conditions of justification, they can be no ministration of death, or killing letter to us."[30]

Human Inability

Although Marshall is clear in his opposition against Antinomianism, he views legalism on the other extreme as a greater danger.[31] As a Pauline divine,[32] Marshall does not have a problem with the law itself. The law is holy (Rom 7:12) and we should conform to it—that is, to love God and to love our neighbor. The consequent question is: What are the effectual means by which "this great excellent end may be accomplished?"[33] For Marshall, a wrong answer to this question is to say "through diligent performance and rushing blindly on immediate practice as if holiness is the means of an end of eternal salvation not as an end itself."[34] He is against any notion that obedience of the law would justify us or make us holy.[35] Marshall argues that our sinfulness will always result in total failure. "We are all, by nature, void of all strength and ability to perform acceptably that holiness and righteousness which the law requires, and are dead."[36]

Marshall shows that the reason for our total inability reverts back to Adam's fall. Before the fall "Adam was made in righteousness, and true holiness and uprightness. Before the fall Adam was not merely able to choose good or evil, but he had bent and propensity of hear to the practice of holiness."[37] However, Adam also had the ability to act contrary to that right inclination. After the fall, Adam lost this original inclination to holiness; thus "he became unable to perform the law of God in the way that

29. Lee, "Sanctification by Faith," 71.
30. Marshall, *Gospel Mystery of Sanctification*, 109.
31. Marshall, *Gospel Mystery of Sanctification*, 107.
32. Whyte, "Appreciation of Walter Marshall," 228.
33. Marshall, *Gospel Mystery of Sanctification*, 5.
34. Marshall, *Gospel Mystery of Sanctification*, 6.
35. Marshall, *Gospel Mystery of Sanctification*, 116.
36. Marshall, *Gospel Mystery of Sanctification*, 6.
37. Marshall, *Gospel Mystery of Sanctification*, 19.

God had designed."[38] Marshall argues that all humanity received this fallen state from the first Adam, and he calls it the natural state that we receive by being born and created in Adam by natural generation.[39] According to this natural state, "we are dead in trespasses and sins, unable to will or do anything that is spiritually good, notwithstanding the redemption that is by Christ until we are actually quickened by Christ (Eph 2:1; Rom 8:7–9)."[40] For Marshall, human beings are naturally lacking the power and will to do good. Therefore, no chance exists for men to become holy if they are left to their corruption. This inability applies to everyone, so that "even those with whom God has begun the good work, if they are left to their corruption, they shall certainly prove vile apostates, and their latter end will be worse than their beginning."[41]

Interestingly, Marshall's teaching about our original state in Adam before the fall and our natural state in Adam after the fall resonates with the teaching of *Westminster Confession of Faith*. In chapter 4 about the creation, the *Confession* teaches that "God furnished Adam with a sufficient knowledge of His will (the law written in his heart, plus a special directive to test his obedience), and that Adam was capable of due obedience but also of falling."[42] The *Confession* moves forward in chapter 6 to explain the fall of Adam and the way that this fall robbed Adam of his original righteousness so that he was no longer holy.[43] Adam's corrupt nature, according to the *Confession*, did not only become his but also was passed on from generation to generation to all human beings.[44] The *Confession* describes this tragedy of humanity by saying that "from this original corruption, whereby we are utterly indisposed, disabled, and made opposite to all good, and wholly inclined to all evil, do proceed all actual transgressions" (WCF 6.4). In a fashion similar to Marshall, the *Confession* emphasizes that man lacks the power to be holy and also lacks the heart to will holiness.

Accordingly, all endeavors to be holy in our natural state are fruitless. Marshall expresses this impossibility of fulfilling the duties of the law by saying, "It is easier to remove a mountain than to move and incline the

---

38. Lee, "Sanctification by Faith," 80–81.
39. Marshall, *Gospel Mystery of Sanctification*, 80.
40. Marshall, *Gospel Mystery of Sanctification*, 35.
41. Marshall, *Gospel Mystery of Sanctification*, 35–36.
42. Williamson, *Westminster Confession of Faith*, 57.
43. Van Dixhoorn, *Confessing the Faith*, 84.
44. Van Dixhoorn, *Confessing the Faith*, 88.

heart to will and affect the doing of them."⁴⁵ For Marshall, "trying to mortify our corrupt nature and begetting a holy frame of heart by striving earnestly to master our sinful lusts is like trying to squeeze oil out of a flint."⁴⁶ Instead, "some endowments or qualifications are needed to produce that holy frame of soul without which the practical life of holiness is impossible."⁴⁷ He argues that "the true way of mortifying sin and quickening ourselves to holiness is by receiving a new nature, out of the fullness of Christ."⁴⁸

Endowments for True Holiness

Marshall denies that our nature after the fall with its evil inclination could ever perform any act of true obedience to the law. Hence, he argues that some endowments are needed to solve the problem of our inability. In direction two of the book, Marshall explains four of these endowments which are necessary means to enable us for the immediate practice of the law.⁴⁹ These four endowments are 1) an inclination to the duties of the law; 2) a persuasion of our reconciliation with God; 3) a persuasion of our future everlasting happiness with God; and finally, 4) a persuasion of sufficient strength both to will and to do God's will acceptably. Marshall believes that these endowments are needed not only in the beginning of the Christian life but also in its continuation. Therefore, "these endowments must continue in us during the present life, or else our ability for a holy life will be lost . . . these endowments must exist before the practice of the holy life as the cause is before the effect."⁵⁰

Adam is a key figure for Marshall in his book. He uses Adam many times in his arguments and the following is one of these occurrences. The first Adam is the first example of a person who "had excellent endowments bestowed on him for a holy practice when he was first created according to the image of God."⁵¹ Marshall uses this example to show how necessary these endowments are for us today. If Adam before the fall with all his privileges needed endowments for a holy practice, how much more do

---

45. Marshall, *Gospel Mystery of Sanctification*, 37.
46. Marshall, *Gospel Mystery of Sanctification*, 42.
47. Murray, "Introduction," 2.
48. Marshall, *Gospel Mystery of Sanctification*, 42.
49. Marshall, *Gospel Mystery of Sanctification*, 14.
50. Marshall, *Gospel Mystery of Sanctification*, 14–15.
51. Marshall, *Gospel Mystery of Sanctification*, 15.

we need these endowments? "Against the powers of darkness, all worldly terrors and allurements, and our own inbred domineering corruptions,"[52] these endowments are indispensable.

Marshall follows a certain pattern while discussing these four endowments. He first gives a brief explanation of the endowment. Then he states what the counter arguments against those endowments are or what the potential adversaries that contradict those endowments are. Finally, he refutes these adversaries by giving different arguments full of scriptural evidences. In his refutation, Marshall opposes both Antinomians and Neonomians, or legalists; however most of his arguments are against the latter.

Marshall sees the four endowments as being strongly connected, though he does not allot them in equal status. For him, the first endowment has precedence over the other three endowments. This certain relation between the four endowments is defined by their nature. The first endowment is the necessity of having a new nature, a new inclination for holy practice. For Marshall, "this propensity is not the same kind of instinctive propensity as some inanimate creatures and animals have for their natural operations."[53] Rather, this propensity is rational as "one is fitting for intelligent creatures, by which they are, by the conduct of reason prone and bent to approve and choose their duty and averse to the practice of sin."[54] Marshall then argues that the other three endowments are the rational tools that make the first endowment not just a blind propensity but a rational one.[55]

Inclination to the Duties of the Law

The first endowment that Marshall asserts is the necessity of possessing a new nature and a new inclination to holiness. This endowment is against the claims of "those who account it sufficient if we have strength to practice holiness if we will, or to will it if we please; and this is the sufficient strength which they earnestly contend for as a great benefit bestowed on all mankind by universal redemption."[56] Marshall's view is in opposition to

---

52. Marshall, *Gospel Mystery of Sanctification*, 15.
53. Marshall, *Gospel Mystery of Sanctification*, 86.
54. Marshall, *Gospel Mystery of Sanctification*, 17.
55. Marshall, *Gospel Mystery of Sanctification*, 17.
56. Marshall, *Gospel Mystery of Sanctification*, 35.

the view of the Arminians who teach that "Christ's death has restored the freedom of the will for all men."[57] They teach that

> Christ, by the merit of His death, has restored that freedom of will to good which was lost by the Fall, and has set nature on its legs again, and that, if they endeavor to do what lies in them, Christ will do the rest, by assisting them with the supplies of His saving grace; so they trust on the grace of Christ to help them in their endeavors.[58]

For Marshall, "the duties of the law are of such a nature that they cannot possibly be performed while there is wholly an aversion or mere indifferency of the heart to the performance of them."[59] The ground that Marshall has for such an impossibility is the inseparableness of fulfilling the law and loving God. To be holy means to love God, to love all his ways and to delight in doing his will.[60] Fulfilling the law is not a matter of just obeying some commandments externally out of fear. For Marshall, such an external obedience of the law is similar "to love our duty only as a market man loves foul ways to the market, or as a sick man loves an unpleasant medicinal potion, or as a captive slave loves his hard work for fear of a greater evil."[61] This kind of obedience is "performed with averseness"[62] which is contrary to the real definition of the law, that is to love God and to love our neighbor.

Moreover, Marshall sees the Arminian claim as false because a state in which man is free to choose between good or evil indifferently does not exist: "Adam did not have a mere power to will to choose between good or evil but he had a propensity to the practice of holiness.... The second Adam also, the Lord Jesus Christ, was born a holy thing (Luke 1:35), with a holy disposition of His soul, and propensity to goodness."[63] After the fall, our inclination turns to sin, which Marshall calls the natural state. This natural state prevents us from the practice of holiness and enslaves us to the practice of sin as long as we possess it.[64] The proposition that man had at one time a mere free will without any kind of inclination never existed.

57. Beeke, "Introduction," xii.
58. Marshall, *Gospel Mystery of Sanctification*, 82.
59. Marshall, *Gospel Mystery of Sanctification*, 18.
60. Marshall, *Gospel Mystery of Sanctification*, 18.
61. Marshall, *Gospel Mystery of Sanctification*, 18.
62. Marshall, *Gospel Mystery of Sanctification*, 18.
63. Marshall, *Gospel Mystery of Sanctification*, 19.
64. Marshall, *Gospel Mystery of Sanctification*, 86.

Accordingly, to return to the life of holiness from which Adam fell or to be imitators of Christ, the second Adam,[65] man needs a new inclination to holiness and not merely free will.

Another argument that Marshall uses for the necessity of this new inclination is the reality of our sinful natural state. This natural state is characterized by properties that make us "dead to God and godliness from the birth."[66] This natural state with all its properties is like a factory that only produces actual sins. Marshall explains these properties as follows:

> The first property is the guilt of sin even of Adam's first sin, and of the sinful depravation of our nature, and of all our own actual transgressions.... Another property is an evil conscience which denounces the wrath of God against us for sin and inclines us to abhor Him as our enemy, rather than to love Him.... A third property is an evil inclination tending only to sin.... A fourth property is subjection to the power of the devil who is the god of this world.[67]

The last argument that Marshall includes in this point is the necessity of taking out the heart of stone and of the giving of a new heart of flesh instead.[68] With the presence of the natural state with all these sinful and miserable properties, the "human will shall be employed only in the service of sin."[69] Only the Son of God by his redemption can set us free from the guilt of sin and from that evil propensity and can give us a new heart. By this gift of a new heart, "we are enabled both to will and to do anything that is acceptable to God."[70]

Therefore, an inclination to love God rather than free will is the solution to our natural state. Our need to attain holiness is greater than mere free will, which was never an option. Marshall argues that holiness can only be attained by the endowment with a new inclination that comes through Christ and his redemptive work. He expresses this thought in the following words:

> Christ aimed at a higher end in His incarnation, death and resurrection, than the restoring the decay and ruins of our natural state.

65. Lee, "Sanctification by Faith," 85.
66. Marshall, *Gospel Mystery of Sanctification*, 20.
67. Marshall, *Gospel Mystery of Sanctification*, 87–88.
68. Marshall, *Gospel Mystery of Sanctification*, 21.
69. Lee, "Sanctification by Faith," 85.
70. Marshall, *Gospel Mystery of Sanctification*, 138.

He aimed to advance us to a new state, more excellent than the state of nature ever was, by union and fellowship with Himself, that we might live to God, not by the power of a natural free will, but by the power of His Spirit living and acting in us. So we may conclude that our natural state is irrecoverable and desperate because Christ, the only Saviour, did not aim at the recovery of it. It is neither holy nor happy, but subject to sin and to all miseries, as long as it remains. Even those that are in a new state in Christ, and do serve the law of God with their mind, do yet with their flesh serve the law of sin (Rom. 7:25).[71]

Persuasion of Our Reconciliation with God

Next, Marshall explains the other three endowments which make our propensity to love God a rational one, that is, to obey God according to knowledge and not just out of zeal.[72] Marshall believes that "holiness is to be promoted by addressing the mind."[73] The second necessary endowment is our persuasion of our reconciliation, which is based on our justification in Christ.[74] In the next chapter, we will discuss in details about Marshall's understanding of the relation between justification and sanctification. However, we will briefly here explain how Marshall argues that our justification is an endowment without which we can never be holy.

In this endowment, Marshall confronts Neonomianism, which argues that sincere obedience to the law has to be a condition to be performed before our actual justification and reconciliation with God.[75] Marshall understands that this Neonomian view rises as a reaction against the Antinomian misuse of the Reformed doctrine of justification. He explains this fear as follows: "Therefore some late divines have thought fit to bring the doctrine of former Protestants concerning justification to their anvil, and to hammer it into another form, that it might be more free from Antinomianism and effectual to secure a holy practice."[76] In Marshall's view, these divines distort the meaning of justification, and their labor to defend holiness is

---

71. Marshall, *Gospel Mystery of Sanctification*, 88–89.
72. Marshall, *Gospel Mystery of Sanctification*, 17.
73. Marshall, "Walter Marshall and the Origins of Sanctification," 36.
74. Lee, "Sanctification by Faith," 86.
75. Marshall, *Gospel Mystery of Sanctification*, 22.
76. Marshall, *Gospel Mystery of Sanctification*, 22.

"vain and pernicious that will only lead to Antinomian profaneness or painted hypocrisy at best."[77]

Marshall argues that what motivates us to obey God lawfully must be our love for him. Our love for God can only be allured by an apprehension of his love towards us,[78] which is, as Lee notes, manifested in the act of free justification.[79] For Marshall, "If our works are not motivated by God's love to us and do not flow out of reconciliation with Him, then we are still at enmity with Him."[80] If we are at enmity with God, then our works will always be out of hatred and fear which is contrary to the very meaning of the law; that is, to love your God from all your heart, soul, and mind. Hence, Marshall argues that "a mispersuasion of God's love to us is, in many, an occasion of licentiousness and not in holiness."[81]

Persuasion of Our Future Everlasting Happiness with God

Not only does the third endowment concur with the previous one, but it is also dependent upon it. Our reconciliation with God causes another persuasion of our future enjoyment of everlasting heavenly happiness.[82] Marshall argues that reconciliation with God necessarily implies persuasion of future happiness. What he adds here is that this persuasion of future happiness is a rational cause that "allures and encourages our sincere obedience."[83]

Against this claim, Marshall refers to objections from two different extremes. On the one hand, "Neonomianism claims that future happiness should be conditioned upon our good works,"[84] otherwise "this persuasion of our own future happiness tends to licentiousness."[85] On the other hand, Antinomianism claims that holding to future happiness as a motivation to happiness is a kind of legalism.[86] Antinomians saw that "if our works

---

77. Marshall, *Gospel Mystery of Sanctification*, 22.
78. Marshall, *Gospel Mystery of Sanctification*, 25.
79. Lee, "Sanctification by Faith," 87.
80. Beeke, "Introduction," ix.
81. Marshall, *Gospel Mystery of Sanctification*, 23.
82. Marshall, *Gospel Mystery of Sanctification*, 30.
83. Marshall, *Gospel Mystery of Sanctification*, 31.
84. Lee, "Sanctification by Faith," 87.
85. Marshall, *Gospel Mystery of Sanctification*, 30.
86. Beeke, "Introduction," ix.

are being allured or stirred up to by the future enjoyment of the heavenly happiness, then these works are legal and mercenary flowing from self-love and not from any pure love to God."[87]

In answering the Neonomian fear, Marshall argues that future happiness and holiness cannot be separated. He asserts,

> This persuasion of our future enjoyment of everlasting happiness cannot tend to licentiousness, if we understand well that perfect holiness is a necessary part of that happiness, and that though we have a title to that happiness by free justification an adoption, yet we must go to the possession of it in a way of holiness (1 John 3:1–3).[88]

Antinomianism rejects this endowment by claiming that if our obedience is motivated by the hope of future happiness, then self-love is the real motive. In response, Marshall makes good use of biblical examples in order to address this objection. He contends that from the beginning, "the sure hope of the glory of heaven is made use of ordinarily by God, since the fall of Adam, as an encouragement to the practice of holiness, as the Scripture abundantly shows."[89] This pattern is evident in the lives of the apostles and in the life of Christ, who was "the great pattern of holiness,"[90] and "who was encouraged to obey for the joy that was set before Him (Heb 12: 2)."[91] Therefore, to be persuaded by future happiness is neither legal nor mercenary, "because the persuasion itself is not gotten by the works of the law, but by free grace through faith (Gal 5: 5)."[92] Marshall does not deny that being moved by the persuasion of future happiness is a kind of a self-love motivation. However, he refuses the notion that this self-love is carnal but views it as a holy self-love.[93] Marshall argues that when we know that God himself is the real prize of that future happiness, then this self-love becomes holy:[94] This self-love is holy because "it inclines us to prefer God above the

---

87. Marshall, *Gospel Mystery of Sanctification*, 31.
88. Marshall, *Gospel Mystery of Sanctification*, 33.
89. Marshall, *Gospel Mystery of Sanctification*, 30.
90. Marshall, *Gospel Mystery of Sanctification*, 32.
91. Beeke, "Introduction," ix.
92. Marshall, *Gospel Mystery of Sanctification*, 34.
93. Marshall, *Gospel Mystery of Sanctification*, 34.
94. Marshall argues that when we see God as our greatest prize and that the heart of our future enjoyment is God himself, then this motivation becomes holy. We obey God now out of love because we are persuaded that in the future God himself will be our

flesh and the world.... And it is far from being contrary to the pure love of God that it brings us to love God more purely and entirely."[95]

Persuasion of Sufficient Strength Both to Will and to Do God's Will Acceptably

The last endowment that is needed so that we might attain the future happiness is a persuasion of sufficient strength, both to will and perform our duty acceptably. In referring to Marshall on sanctification, James Hervey talks about this endowment by saying "a persuasion that God will give us sufficient strength is the point we plead for, the privileges to which we stand entitled by the gospel."[96] Again, Marshall begins by showing the errors that are related to this endowment. Two errors are in view here. First, the Arminian error that claims that "it is sufficient for the practice of holiness to obtain the freedom of the will by the universal redemption of Christ."[97] The second error is the Neonomian teaching,[98] that the practice of godliness is easy, and that what God requires from us is just to do our best.[99]

Marshall answers these objections by pointing to the misery of our natural state. Our natural sinful state lacks the power and the will to do any good. Marshall also refuses any notion that man's endeavors for holy practices are to be accounted sufficient holiness, because man's ability is not the measure of acceptable duty but God's law is the true measure.[100] For Marshall, conformity to the law is never an easy task because conformity does not only mean "to alter vicious customs, but to mortify corrupt natural affections which bred these customs."[101] Accordingly, God must work within man both to will and to do what is pleasing to him. In this fourth endowment, "God furnishes people with a rational persuasion of a sufficient strength so that they may be enabled both to will and to do their duties of the law."[102] Marshall contends that to will and to do what is pleasing to God

---

greatest prize which is in itself an expression of loving God.
    95. Marshall, *Gospel Mystery of Sanctification*, 34.
    96. Hervey, "Letter CIV on Marshall on Sanctification," 334–35.
    97. Lee, "Sanctification by Faith," 88.
    98. Lee, "Sanctification by Faith," 88.
    99. Marshall, *Gospel Mystery of Sanctification*, 35.
    100. Marshall, *Gospel Mystery of Sanctification*, 38.
    101. Marshall, *Gospel Mystery of Sanctification*, 36.
    102. Lee, "Sanctification by Faith," 89.

is a miracle that requires us to know that we have the needed strength to perform it. Therefore, "God encourages his people to discover that strength, which then rationally encourages them to pursue what Marshall called the wonderful enterprise of holiness."[103]

Union and Faith

For Marshall, the endowments discussed in the previous section are the means needed to attain holiness. The question now is: How can we get these endowments? Marshall answers this question in chapters 3 and 4 which are the core of his work.[104] In chapter 3, Marshall shows how the union with Christ is the source through which "the needed endowments for living holily, the heart's inclination, and the sufficient strength to serve God acceptably are provided for us."[105] Then chapter 4 treats faith as the means by which this union is affected.

Marshall believes that although the doctrine of union with Christ is central in our sanctification and is revealed in Scripture, yet the natural man cannot comprehend it and even many godly men may still see this doctrine as a riddle.[106] Two mysteries are in view here in Marshall's mind. The first mystery is concerned with Christ as the source of godliness and holiness, and the second mystery is concerned with the nature of the mystical union between Christ and the believers.

Christ: Source of Holiness

Marshall challenges the common misunderstanding about how we produce holiness in our lives. He is not synergistic in his view of sanctification: "We don't work with Christ in producing holiness but we receive holiness from Christ."[107] Marshall explains this idea by saying that "we are not at all to work together with Christ, in making or producing that holy frame in us, but only to take it to ourselves, and use it in our holy practice, as made

---

103. Beeke, "Introduction," ix.
104. Murray, "Introduction," 2.
105. Murray, "Introduction," 2.
106. Marshall, *Gospel Mystery of Sanctification*, 40.
107. Beeke, "Introduction," x.

JUSTIFICATION, SANCTIFICATION, AND UNION WITH CHRIST

ready to our hands."[108] For Marshall, this reality is a great mystery because it is against the common thinking that "we must get a holy frame by producing it anew in ourselves and by forming and working it out of our own hearts."[109]

Marshall makes the comparison between Adam and Christ, as he is used to doing to show that "as our corruption was produced in the first Adam, then passed on to us, so our holiness is first produced in Christ, then passed on to us."[110] Therefore, "the holy frame and disposition, by which our souls are furnished and enabled for immediate practice of the law, must be obtained by receiving it out of Christ's fullness, as a thing already prepared and brought to an existence for us in Christ and treasured up in Him."[111] Misunderstanding this mystery would result in "bitter agony and a great deal of misspent burdensome labor,"[112] as people endeavor and struggle to produce this new nature instead of receiving it out of the fullness of Christ.[113]

To elaborate on this argument, Marshall uses two strategies. First, he gives many scriptural evidences. Second, "he highlights the importance of three major events in Christ's earthly life: incarnation, crucifixion and resurrection,"[114] to prepare and form a holy nature for us in himself. Marshall first contends that the Scripture testifies clearly that Christ is the source of our salvation. In some texts we find that "all things pertaining to our salvation are treasured in Christ and comprehended in his fullness,"[115] such as Col 1:19; 2:11–13; Eph 1:3; and 1 Cor 1:30. Marshall goes on to say that "other texts of Scripture show plainly that we receive our holiness out of His fullness be fellowship with Him (John 1:16, 17)."[116]

Then Marshall explains how the three major events in Christ's life play their roles in our sanctification. In Christ's incarnation, "a man was created

---

108. Marshall, *Gospel Mystery of Sanctification*, 41.
109. Marshall, *Gospel Mystery of Sanctification*, 41.
110. Beeke, "Introduction," x.
111. Marshall, *Gospel Mystery of Sanctification*, 41.
112. Marshall, *Gospel Mystery of Sanctification*, 42.
113. Marshall argues that as we are justified by Christ's righteousness worked out by him and imputed to us, so we are sanctified by holiness accomplished in Christ then imparted to us. More discussion on the relation between justification and sanctification will be addressed in the next chapter.
114. Lee, "Sanctification by Faith," 91.
115. Marshall, *Gospel Mystery of Sanctification*, 48.
116. Marshall, *Gospel Mystery of Sanctification*, 49.

in a new holy frame far more excellent than ever the first Adam."[117] The reason for this excellency is that Christ was not a mere man; but, furthermore, he was Emmanuel, God with us. In Christ, we see the inseparable union of the divine and human nature in one person. "The fullness of the Godhead, with all holiness, did first dwell in Him bodily even in His human nature."[118] One end of this glorious union is that "Christ might communicate this excellent frame to His seed that should be born of Him and in Him by His Spirit,"[119] Marshall argues. Therefore, "this perfect union of divine and human nature reveals the prototype or model of the same Christ working within believers for their sanctification."[120] Marshall concludes this point by saying, "Thus He came down from heaven as living bread that, as He lives by the Father, so those that eat Him may live in Him (John 6:51, 56), by the same life of God in them that was first in Him."[121]

Moreover, Marshall refers to Christ's crucifixion to argue that a new nature is communicated to us by his death. For Marshall, Christ's death freed us from the guilt of sin and from our whole natural condition as well. He says:

> He freed Himself from the guilt of our sins imputed to Him and from all that innocent weakness of His human nature which he had borne for our sake. And by freeing himself, he prepared a freedom for us, from our whole natural condition. . . . Thus, the corrupt natural estate, which is called in Scripture the old man, was crucified together with Christ, that the body of sin might be destroyed. And it is destroyed in us, not by any wounds that we ourselves can give to it, but by our partaking of that freedom from it, and death to it, that is already wrought out for us by the death of Christ.[122]

For Marshall, we wrongly think that Christ's death was for our justification only but that our holiness is a task for us to achieve. Instead, he says, "Christ died, not that we might be able to form a holy nature in ourselves,

---

117. Marshall, *Gospel Mystery of Sanctification*, 52.
118. Marshall, *Gospel Mystery of Sanctification*, 52.
119. Marshall, *Gospel Mystery of Sanctification*, 52.
120. Lee, "Sanctification by Faith," 92.
121. Marshall, *Gospel Mystery of Sanctification*, 52.
122. Marshall, *Gospel Mystery of Sanctification*, 52–53.

but that we might receive one ready prepared and formed in Christ for us, by union and fellowship with Him."[123]

Finally, Marshall refers to Christ's resurrection. Marshall says that "He [Christ] took possession of spiritual life for us, as now fully procured for us, and made to be our right and property by the merit of His death."[124] For Marshall, "Christ's resurrection was our resurrection to the life of holiness, as Adam's fall was our fall into spiritual death."[125] By union with Christ, we partake of that spiritual life that he took possession for us at his resurrection.

In conclusion, Marshall sees Christ's incarnation, death, and resurrection as events through which Christ guaranteed spiritual life, or a holy frame, for us. We are not able to work with Christ to produce this holy frame in our lives with the end that we can obey God out of love. Rather, we need to have this spiritual life already completed in Christ for us. This holy frame can be imparted to us by mystical union with him, and "thereby we are enabled to bring forth its fruit of holiness in our daily lives."[126]

Mystical Union

The second mystery that Marshall explains in our sanctification is the mystical union with Christ by which we receive all the treasures that are in Christ. What Marshall means by this mystical union is "a close union as that we are one spirit and one flesh with Him."[127] Marshall's use of the word "mystical" is based on the scriptural reference to this union in Ephesians 5:23 as a great mystery. For Marshall, this union between Christ and the believer is one of three mystical unions presented in Scripture, in addition to the union between the three persons of the Trinity and the union of the divine and human nature of Christ.[128] According to Marshall, "Scripture speaks most of the union between Christ and the believer."[129] The evidence that this union is the most spoken of is the various resemblances used to

---

123. Marshall, *Gospel Mystery of Sanctification*, 54.
124. Marshall, *Gospel Mystery of Sanctification*, 54.
125. Marshall, *Gospel Mystery of Sanctification*, 54.
126. Lee, "Sanctification by Faith," 94.
127. Marshall, *Gospel Mystery of Sanctification*, 43.
128. Marshall, *Gospel Mystery of Sanctification*, 43.
129. Beeke, "Introduction," x.

illustrate it. Marshall lists seven of these resemblances briefly in which our union with Christ is

> (i) as Christ lived in our nature by the Father (John 6:57); (ii) as we receive original sin and death propagated to us from the first Adam (Rom. 5:12, 14, 16, 17); (iii) as the natural body receives sense, motion and nourishment from the head (Col. 2:19); (iv) as the branch receives its sap, juice and fructifying virtue from the vine (John 15:4, 5); (v) as the wife brings forth fruit by virtue of her conjugal union with her husband (Rom. 7:4); (vi) as stones become a holy temple by being built on the foundation, and joined with the chief corner-stone (1 Peter 2:4–6); (vii) as we receive the nourishing virtue of bread by eating it, and of wine by drinking it (John 6:51, 55, 57), which last resemblance is used to seal to us our communion with Christ in the Lord's Supper.[130]

In all these resemblances, Marshall argues that they resonate the pattern in which "all of them intimate that our new life and holy nature are first in Christ, and then in us, by a true proper union and fellowship with Him."[131]

Marshall does not only explain what union with Christ means but also guards the doctrine from possible errors. John Marshall describes Walter Marshall as a person who "is always keen to avoid being misconstrued."[132] Although Marshall refers to different errors that need to be avoided, all these errors can be traced back either to an Antinomian root or to a Neonomian root. Against both errors, Marshall argues that our union with Christ is real and spiritual. While arguing for the spiritual presence of Christ in the elements of the Lord's supper, he says,

> Though Christ is in heaven, and we on earth, yet He can join our souls and bodies to His at such a distance without any substantial change of either, by the same infinite Spirit dwelling in Him and us; and so our flesh will become His, when it is quickened by His Spirit; and His flesh ours, as truly as if we ate His flesh and drank His blood.[133]

Against Antinomianism, Marshall rejects the notion that believers are made God by that mystical union, but only the temple of God. In other

---

130. Marshall, *Gospel Mystery of Sanctification*, 50.
131. Marshall, *Gospel Mystery of Sanctification*, 51.
132. Marshall, "Walter Marshall and the Origins of Sanctification," 24.
133. Marshall, *Gospel Mystery of Sanctification*, 44.

words, Marshall argues that union with Christ is a spiritual union, "in which the union is not of essence, which would result in a confusion of personhood."[134] Furthermore, Marshall opposes the Antinomian view that "since we are in union with Christ, our good works are meaningless." He rejects that the believers could become perfect in holiness, or that Christ could be made a sinner.[135] "Christ knows how to dwell in believers by certain measures and degrees, and to make them holy so far only as He dwells in them."[136]

Once more, we see that Marshall's concern about Neonomianism surpasses his concern about Antinomianism, as shown by the space he gives to refute the Neonomian error. As a reaction against the Antinomian errors, Neonomians go to the opposite direction by mitigating the meaning of union with Christ. Marshall describes their fear when he says,

> Thus that great mystery, the union of believers with Christ Himself—which is the glory of the church, and has been highly owned formerly, both by the ancient fathers, and many eminent Protestant divines ... is now exploded out of the new model of divinity. The reason of exploding it, as I judge in charity, is not because our learned refiners of divinity think themselves less able to defend it than the other two mysterious unions, and to silence the objections of those proud sophisters that will not believe what they cannot comprehend; but rather, because they account it to be one of the sinews of Antinomianism, that lay unobserved in the former usual doctrine; that it tends to puff up men with a persuasion that they are justified and have eternal life in them already, and that they do not need to depend any longer on their uncertain performances of the condition of sincere obedience for salvation; by which they account the very foundation of a holy practice to be subverted.[137]

In answering both errors, Marshall contends that union with Christ is not a result of our obedience nor a license for licentiousness. Rather, union with Christ is "a privilege bestowed on believers in their very first entrance into a holy state, on which all ability to do good works depends, and all sincere obedience to the law follows after it, as fruit produced by it."[138] Marshall's approach to the vital doctrine of union with Christ is a careful one.

---

134. Lee, "Sanctification by Faith," 100.
135. Beeke, "Introduction," x.
136. Marshall, *Gospel Mystery of Sanctification*, 45.
137. Marshall, *Gospel Mystery of Sanctification*, 46–47.
138. Marshall, *Gospel Mystery of Sanctification*, 47.

Cheul Hee Lee argues that "for Marshall, far from being a threat to the life of holiness, union with Christ was the only way that makes one enabled to practice the law properly as required by God."[139]

The Holy Spirit and Union

What makes the union real and spiritual is the work of the Holy Spirit. Marshall argues that the same Holy Spirit that rested on Christ in all fullness is also communicated from him to us, thus forming the union between the believers and Christ.[140] Through this work of the Holy Spirit, the believer realizes this union with Christ.[141] For Marshall, to have Christ himself and to have the Spirit of Christ is similar since the Spirit is the one who joins us to Christ "as the great bond of union."[142] Therefore, Marshall asserts that "our sanctification is by the Holy Spirit,"[143] because by the presence of the Spirit of Christ in us, "He inclines us to mind spiritual things at to lust against the flesh (Rom 8:1, 4, 5; Gal 5:17)."[144]

Marshall is also keen to avoid any division in the covenant between the Old Testament and New Testament.[145] He argues that sanctification of the saints of the Old Testament was through the same means of union with Christ even before the incarnation. Marshall explains this idea, when he says, "This Spirit was able and effectual to unite those saints to that flesh which Christ was to take to Himself in the fullness of time, because He was the same in both, and to give out to them that grace with which Christ would afterwards fill His flesh, for their salvation as well as ours."[146]

Again, we find that Marshall's ideas resonates with the ideas of Calvin. For the reformer, all salvific blessings, including sanctification, become ours through union with Christ. Calvin says in his *Institutes*: "First, we must understand that as long as Christ remains outside of us, and we are separated from him, all that he has suffered and done for the salvation of the human

---

139. Lee, "Sanctification by Faith," 97–98.
140. Marshall, *Gospel Mystery of Sanctification*, 55.
141. Beeke, "Introduction," xi.
142. Marshall, *Gospel Mystery of Sanctification*, 55.
143. Marshall, *Gospel Mystery of Sanctification*, 54.
144. Marshall, *Gospel Mystery of Sanctification*, 56.
145. Marshall, "Walter Marshall and the Origins of Sanctification," 25.
146. Marshall, *Gospel Mystery of Sanctification*, 57.

race remains useless and of no value for us."[147] Regarding sanctification and how it relies on union with Christ, Calvin believes that "by the power of his [Christ's] Spirit, he makes us a part of his body, so that from him we derive our life."[148] Calvin comments on Rom 6:5 and says that being united to Christ does not only designate "a conformity of example, but a secret union, by which we are joined to him; so that he, reviving us by his Spirit, transfers his own virtue to us."[149] In this quotation, we see how Calvin and Marshall are similar in their views on sanctification and union with Christ. For both, our sanctification flows from the mystical union with Christ that is actualized by the work of the Holy Spirit through whom Christ's holiness is communicated to us.

Marshall's teaching about union with Christ and sanctification has also some resemblance to the documents of the Westminster Assembly. In the answer to question 69 in the *Larger Catechism*, sanctification is strongly attached to union with Christ:[150] "The communion in grace which the members of the invisible church have with Christ, is their partaking of the virtue of his mediation, in their justification, adoption, sanctification, and whatever else, in this life, manifests their union with him." Although the *Westminster Confession* does not use the word "union" in chapter 13 about sanctification, it is strongly implied. The first sentence in that chapter states, "They, who are once effectually called, and regenerated, having a new heart, and a new spirit created in them, are further sanctified, really and personally, through the virtue of Christ's death and resurrection, by His Word and Spirit dwelling in them." Resonating with Calvin, one of the proof texts used is Rom 6:5, 6, which refers directly to union with Christ as the only way to be dead to sin. For the Assembly, sanctification was found in union with Christ, like every Christian blessing and benefit.[151]

To conclude, Marshall's book makes union with Christ the starting point in the Christian life.[152] In union with Christ, the believer shares all the blessings treasured in Christ that he accomplished in his life, death, and resurrection. Marshall points out that this union is the means through which we can live for God. Marshall concludes,

147. Calvin, *Inst.* 3.1.1.
148. Calvin, *Calvin's Commentaries*, Eph 5:31.
149. Calvin, *Calvin's Commentaries*, Rom 6:5.
150. *Westminster Larger Catechism*, question 69.
151. Van Dixhoorn, *Confessing the Faith*, 178.
152. Murray, "Introduction," 3.

The effectual causes of those four principal endowments, which in the foregoing direction were asserted as necessary to furnish us for the immediate practice of holiness, are comprehended in the fullness of Christ, and treasured up for us in Him; and the endowments themselves, together with their causes, are attained richly by union and fellowship with Christ.[153]

What Is Faith?

We have already discussed the way that Marshall views faith in relation with justification. In this section, more light will be shed on the way Marshall relates faith to union with Christ and sanctification. For Marshall, the Spirit is the one who accomplishes our union with Christ. However, this accomplishment occurs by the use of two means: the gospel and faith.[154] First, God reveals the glory of Christ for us in the gospel and "invites us and commands us to believe on Christ for salvation and encourages us by a free promise of that salvation to all that believe on Him."[155] The second means is faith, which is our instrument of reception by which our mystical union with Christ is accomplished.[156] The question raised here is: How can a natural man whose natural tendency is hostility to God, ever be able to exercise faith by which union with Christ may happen? This question becomes more pressing when we remember that Marshall already teaches that no holy endowment, including faith, can ever exist without the mystical union with Christ. The real question is: Does faith precede union with Christ, or the other way around?[157]

Before answering this question, Marshall shows his consistency when he argues that "we shall never come to Christ by any teaching of man, except we also hear and learn of the Father and be drawn to Christ by His Spirit,"[158] Then Marshall gives a helpful explanation to solve that dilemma. He argues that the Spirit, first, "works saving faith in us and answers the aim and end of that faith by giving us union and fellowship with Christ by

---

153. Marshall, *Gospel Mystery of Sanctification*, 55.
154. Marshall, *Gospel Mystery of Sanctification*, 59.
155. Marshall, *Gospel Mystery of Sanctification*, 60.
156. Marshall, *Gospel Mystery of Sanctification*, 60–61.
157. Beeke and Jones, *Puritan Theology*, 484.
158. Marshall, *Gospel Mystery of Sanctification*, 76.

it."[159] According to Marshall's idea, "Before the new believer is aware our Lord unites us to Himself (takes hold of us) and works in us. The Spirit then regenerates the sinner, who in turn exercises faith toward Christ and completes the union."[160] "Thus, we are first passive, and then active, in this great work of mystical union; we are first apprehended of Christ, and then we apprehend Christ."[161]

Marshall's explanation of this dynamics between our faith and union with Christ is not unique. A great similarity to his view is evident in the writings of Thomas Goodwin (1600–1680). In Goodwin's *The Object and Act of Justifying Faith*, he argues that Christ initiates the union with the sinner, "yet this union is only complete when that sinner exercises faith in Christ."[162] Goodwin argues that "the union on Christ's part is in order of nature first made by the Spirit; therefore, Philip. iii. 12, he is said first to 'comprehend us ere we can comprehend him'; yet that which makes the union on our part is faith."[163] In another instance, Goodwin also speaks of "the act of the will by which the union on our parts completed between Christ and us, and we are thereby made ultimately with him."[164] Marshall gives a helpful illustration to explain this idea by saying that "Christ entered first into the soul, to join Himself to it, by giving it the spirit of faith; and so the soul receives Christ and His Spirit by their own power; as the sun first enlightens our eyes, and then we can see it by its own light."[165]

By this explanation, Marshall shows that "faith does not unite us to Christ by its own virtue, but by the power of the Spirit working by it and with it."[166] Hence, faith is not considered as a conditional work for one's union with Christ, but it is the instrument by which the Holy Spirit accomplishes the union with Christ. Accordingly, all the glory belongs to Christ and the Spirit for our mystical union with Christ and nothing belongs to our faith. However, all spiritual blessings treasured in Christ, including sanctification can only flow to us when our union with Christ is complete by the exercise of faith. Therefore, Marshall sees faith as "the uniting grace

---

159. Marshall, *Gospel Mystery of Sanctification*, 77.
160. Beeke and Jones, *Puritan Theology*, 485.
161. Marshall, *Gospel Mystery of Sanctification*, 77.
162. Beeke and Jones, *Puritan Theology*, 485.
163. Goodwin, "Object and Acts of Justifying Faith," 463.
164. Goodwin, "Object and Acts of Justifying Faith," 273.
165. Marshall, *Gospel Mystery of Sanctification*, 77.
166. Marshall, *Gospel Mystery of Sanctification*, 77.

by which the Spirit of God knits the knot of mystical marriage between Christ and us."¹⁶⁷ At the same time, he sees faith as "the duty with which a holy life is to begin, and by which the foundation of all other holy duties is laid in the soul."¹⁶⁸ Marshall's conclusion to chapter 4 is a helpful summary of this point when he says,

> And, no doubt, Christ is thus united to many infants who have the spirit of faith and yet cannot act faith, because they are not come to the use of their understandings; but those of riper years that are joined passively to Christ by the spirit of faith will also join themselves with Him actively, by the act of faith and, until they act this faith, they cannot know or enjoy their union with Christ and the comfort of it, or make use of it in acting any other duties of holiness acceptably in this life.¹⁶⁹

Another important idea about faith for Marshall is that "saving faith must necessarily contain two acts, believing the truth of the gospel, and believing on Christ, as promised freely to us in the gospel, for all salvation."¹⁷⁰ Marshall argues that faith is concerned with believing the gospel as the most excellent truth and also with receiving Christ himself with a similar heartiness for salvation. He gives a helpful illustration for the two acts of faith: "It is one act to receive the breast or cup in which milk or wine are conveyed, and another act to suck the milk in the breast and to drink the wine in the cup."¹⁷¹ These two acts are inseparable in Marshall's thinking, "the one without the other would not accomplish the saving purpose of faith."¹⁷² For Marshall, faith receives Christ himself as we receive the wine in the cup. Marshall goes on to say,

> And the Scripture illustrates this receiving by the similitude of eating and drinking: He that believes on Christ drinks the living water of His Spirit (John 7:37–39). Christ is the bread of life; His flesh is meat indeed, and His blood is drink indeed. And the way to eat and drink it is to believe in Christ and, by so doing, we dwell

---

167. Marshall, *Gospel Mystery of Sanctification*, 193.
168. Marshall, *Gospel Mystery of Sanctification*, 193.
169. Marshall, *Gospel Mystery of Sanctification*, 78.
170. Marshall, *Gospel Mystery of Sanctification*, 61.
171. Marshall, *Gospel Mystery of Sanctification*, 61.
172. Lee, "Sanctification by Faith," 110.

in Christ, and Christ in us, and we have everlasting life (John 6:35, 47, 48, 54–56).[173]

Marshall believes that the faith in its essence is designed for the purpose of union with Christ and sanctification. He goes on to say that "by the very act of hearty trusting or believing on Christ for salvation and happiness, the soul casts and puts away from itself everything that keeps it at a distance from Christ."[174] Our confidence is totally placed in Christ instead of anything that pertains to us. Another important aspect of the nature of saving faith is that it has a natural tendency to furnish the soul with a holy frame and nature, and all endowments necessary to it, out of the fullness of Christ.[175] When we comprehend all the salvific blessings that we have in Christ, we are "heartily disposed and mightily strengthened for the practice of holiness."[176] Thirdly, "because faith has such a natural tendency to dispose and strengthen the soul for the practice of holiness, we have cause to judge it a suitable instrument to accomplish every part of that practice in an acceptable manner."[177] Consequently, faith promotes sanctification; as in its essence, faith contains love, trust, and dependence for Christ with all his holiness. Marshall concludes:

> By faith we live and act in all good works, as people in Christ, as raised above ourselves, and in our natural state, by partaking of Him and His salvation; and we do all in His name and on His account. This is the practice of that mysterious manner of living to God in holiness which is peculiar to the Christian religion in which we live; and yet not we, but Christ lives in us (Gal. 2:20).[178]

The way Marshall handles the relation between faith and sanctification also refutes the errors of both Neonomianism and Antinomianism. On the one hand, the faith he describes "roots and grounds us in holiness, more than the mere accepting of any terms of salvation and consenting to have Christ for our Lord can do."[179] On the other hand, Marshall refuses the Neonomian notion that faith is not enough for the practice of holiness.

---

173. Marshall, *Gospel Mystery of Sanctification*, 68.
174. Marshall, *Gospel Mystery of Sanctification*, 70.
175. We will expand more on this point in the next chapter on the relation between justification and sanctification.
176. Marshall, *Gospel Mystery of Sanctification*, 73.
177. Marshall, *Gospel Mystery of Sanctification*, 73.
178. Marshall, *Gospel Mystery of Sanctification*, 74.
179. Marshall, *Gospel Mystery of Sanctification*, 74.

Neonomians argue that relying on faith alone would lead to licentiousness. In answering them, Marshall argues that the faith that is not holy is a dead faith, and that true faith should not be blamed for the misuse of the word faith. True faith is "more powerful to secure a holy practice than any of those resolutions of obedience, or resigning acts, that some would have to be the great conditions of our salvation, which are indeed no better than hypocritical acts, if they are not produced by this faith."[180]

Conclusion

In conclusion, Marshall's of view of the total inability of human nature after the fall, destroys any hope of proper obedience to God's law in our natural state. A new inclination or propensity is required in order that we may live in holiness and proper obedience to God's law. This new state that bears the fruits of holiness is only possible through union with Christ by the instrumentality of faith. Marshall's idea can be summarized in these words:

> Let them learn here that the old and new man are two contrary states, containing in them, not only sin and holiness, but all other things that dispose and incline us to the practice of them; and that the old man must be put off, as crucified with Christ, before we can be freed from the practice of sin (Rom. 6:6, 7). And therefore we cannot lead a new life until we have first got a new state by faith in Christ.[181]

Marshall understands that sanctification is a lifelong process in which our faith in Christ increases, and hence our holiness increases. He urges the believers to "continue and increase in their most holy faith, that so their enjoyment of Christ, union and fellowship with Him, and all holiness by Him, may be begun, continued and increased in them."[182] Andrew Murray, who was an editor worthy of Walter Marshall,[183] gives a helpful, concise description of Marshall's teaching on sanctification in the following words:

> Jesus Christ and the holy nature there is in Him for us is so fully set forth; faith as the means of receiving that holy nature in its Divine power and efficacy, to enable us in all things to live a holy life, is

---

180. Marshall, *Gospel Mystery of Sanctification*, 74.
181. Marshall, *Gospel Mystery of Sanctification*, 86.
182. Marshall, *Gospel Mystery of Sanctification*, 193.
183. Whyte, "Appreciation of Walter Marshall," 229.

made so clear; the Father's will and expectation that we should indeed live such a life, in accordance with the sufficient provision He has made, is so brought home that the earnest reader cannot but learn to understand better how we can indeed live holy lives by abiding in Christ, our holiness.[184]

---

184. Murray, "Introduction," 7.

CHAPTER 5

Walter Marshall
Power of the Gospel and Spiritual Growth

"It is written, 'YOU SHALL BE HOLY, FOR I AM HOLY'" said the apostle Peter in his first epistle (1 Pet 1:16). This call to holiness is part and parcel of Christianity. No Christian would debate the necessity of holiness for Christians; however, the debates arise when we think of the means to become holy.[1] The question to be asked here is: How is holiness related to our relation to God? Do we become holy in order to establish our relationship with God, or do we become holy as a result of our reconciled relationship with God? Is holiness a means to an end or is holiness itself an end? Walter Marshall comments on this last question by showing how a person may misunderstand the place of holiness in the Christian life. He argues, "They look on holiness as only the means of an end, of eternal salvation: not as an end itself, requiring any great means for attaining the practice of it. The enquiry of most, when they begin to have a sense of religion, is 'What good thing shall I do, that I may have eternal life?' (Matt. 19:16); not, 'How shall I be enabled to do anything that is good?'"[2]

Another way to grapple with how holiness and the relation to God relates is through the two technical words, "justification" and "sanctification." In the last two chapters, we dealt with Marshall's teaching on each of these two terms separately. Marshall holds to a traditional Reformed view of both

---

1. McRae, "Introduction," 6.
2. Marshall, *Gospel Mystery of Sanctification*, 6.

justification and sanctification. In line with Reformed theology, "justification is understood, forensically, to indicate the act of God in declaring the sinner to be free from all legal charge, on account of the satisfaction made by Christ on his behalf; and sanctification is that act of God by which the believer's life is transformed more and more after a godly pattern."[3]

As mentioned earlier, Marshall lived in a context in which both Antinomianism and Neonomianism were actively distorting the meanings of justification and sanctification. Marshall was keen to answer such errors by giving both justification and sanctification their accurate meaning and by explaining the proper relationship between these two graces. In the current chapter, more light will be shed on the way that both justification and sanctification relate in Marshall's theology. Understanding this relation is crucial, especially in light of the errors that arise as a result of confusing justification and sanctification.

False Views

The relation between justification and sanctification is controversial. In understanding this relation, Marshall points out different errors that may arise in this area. For instance, Marshall refers in his sermon on justification to the Papists' error in which they confounded justification and sanctification together.[4] The Papists' error was that "they made sanctification into justification."[5] For them, to be justified means to be perfect inherently by infusion of grace. Marshall refuses this understanding of justification and insists that justification is a juridical word. He contends that "justification is not a real change of a sinner in himself (though a real change is annexed to it) but only a relative change with reference to God's judgment."[6]

Another form of mixing justification and sanctification is Antinomianism. Although Antinomians glorify the work of Christ for justification, they fail to understand the proper relationship between law and grace.[7] Marshall comments on their error by saying that "they account it a part of the liberty from the bondage of the law, purchased by the blood of Christ,

---

3. Kevan, *Grace of Law*, 95.
4. Marshall, "Doctrine of Justification Opened," 2.
5. Kevan, *Grace of Law*, 99.
6. Marshall, "Doctrine of Justification Opened," 4.
7. Kevan, *Grace of Law*, 24.

to make no conscience of breaking the law in their conversation."[8] Antinomianism downplays the importance of sanctification and good works. J. I. Packer comments on the Antinomian error: "Instead of putting sin out of life, the Antinomian seeks to remove sin out of mind. Accordingly, repentance becomes unnecessary for assurance, and good works unnecessary for heaven."[9] Contrary to the Papists, "Antinomians made justification into sanctification."[10] Therefore, on one hand, the Papists deny all the comforts that are in our justification in Christ. On the other hand, the Antinomians abuse the comforts of justification and downplayed the importance of holiness in our lives.

In reaction to Antinomianism and as a result of the fear of licentiousness, Neonomianism appeared "to introduce a doctrine of justification by obedience to a new law."[11] In promoting Neonomianism, "Richard Baxter (1615–91) was both a bitter opponent of Antinomianism and one of the principal architects of Neonomianism."[12] Baxter differentiates between two kinds of justification. First, he refers to "an initial justification in which our works do not play any role."[13] With regard to the second kind, Baxter points to "the ultimate justification of the believer which is achieved by a combination of the merit of Christ and the believer's own good works in obedience to the new law."[14] Baxter's teaching of twofold justification demands two forms of righteousness: a legal righteousness and an evangelical righteousness. For Baxter, Christ's performance achieved universal legal righteousness which is imputed to us by faith. However, this universal righteousness becomes ours by way of a condition, which is our particular evangelical righteousness.[15] Baxter does not place Christ's righteousness and man's righteousness on the same level. "He acknowledges that the death of Christ is the sole ground of God's acceptance of the believer's good works."[16] However, our personal righteousness is the necessary subordinate

---

8. Marshall, *Gospel Mystery of Sanctification*, 148.
9. Packer, *Redemption & Restoration of Man*, 365–66.
10. Kevan, *Grace of Law*, 99.
11. Kevan, *Grace of Law*, 204.
12. Marshall, "Walter Marshall and the Origins of Sanctification," 21.
13. Boersma, *Hot Pepper Corn*, 293.
14. Kevan, *Grace of Law*, 205.
15. Boersma, *Hot Pepper Corn*, 283.
16. Kevan, *Grace of Law*, 206.

condition,[17] which gives us the right to Christ's righteousness that is our sole ground for acceptance before God.[18] Baxter illustrates his view in the metaphor of the "pepper corn" in his *Alphorismes*:

> A Tenant forfeiteth his Lease to his Landlord, by not paying his rent; he runs deep in debt to him, and is disabled to pay him any more rent for the future, whereupon he is put out of his house, and cast into prison, till he pay the debt; his Landlords son payeth it for him, taketh him out of prison, and putteth him in his house again, as his Tenant, having purchased house and all to himself; he maketh him a new Lease in this Tenor, that paying but a *pepper corn* yearly to him, he shall be acquit both from his debt, and from all other rent for the future, which by his old Lease was to be paid; yet doth he not cancel the old lease, but keepeth it in his hands to put in suite against the Tenant, if he should be so foolish as to deny the payment of the *pepper corn*. In this case the payment of the grain of pepper is imputed to Tenant, as if he had payed the rent of the old Lease: yet this imputation doth not extol the *pepper corn*, nor vilifie the benefit of his Benefactor, who redeemed him: nor can it be said, that the purchase did only serve to advance the value and efficacy of that grain of pepper.[19]

Baxter asserts that we cannot attribute our evangelical righteousness to Christ. Furthermore, he contends that this evangelical righteousness is inevitable for our ultimate justification. Baxter argues, "To affirm therefore that our Evangelical or New Covenant-Righteousness is in Christ, and not in ourselves, or performed by Christ, and not by ourselves is such a monstrous piece of Antinomian doctrine."[20] Marshall completely rejects Baxter's teaching. Although Baxter's name does not appear in Marshall's book, "Marshall strongly attacks Baxter's teaching, or if not specifically Baxter, yet he attacks those who derived their views from Baxter."[21] He sees the error of Neonomianism as a republication of the Papists' error. For instance, in reference to Neonomianism, Marshall states:

> But I hope to show that this their imagined sure foundation of holiness was never laid by the holy God, but that it is rather an error in the foundation, pernicious to the true faith, and to holiness

---

17. Boersma, *Hot Pepper Corn*, 285.
18. Kevan, *Grace of Law*, 206.
19. Baxter, *Aphorismes*, 127–28. Italics are mine.
20. Baxter, *Aphorismes*, 111.
21. Marshall, "Walter Marshall and the Origins of Sanctification," 19.

of life. I account it an error especially to be abhorred and detested, because we are so prone to be seduced by it, and because it is an error by which Satan, transforming himself into an angel of light, and a patron of holiness, has greatly withstood the gospel in the apostles' times, and stirred up men to persecute it out of zeal for the law, and has since prevailed to set and maintain Popery, by which the mystery of iniquity works apace in these days to corrupt the purity of the gospel among Protestants, and to heal the deadly wound that was given to Popery by preaching the doctrine of justification by faith without works.[22]

Marshall sees Baxter's way of defending holiness is in itself "destructive to the means of holiness and to holiness itself."[23] For Marshall, the Neonomian teaching is satanic, as it prevents many poor souls from coming to Christ. Instead, it urges them to keep looking within themselves for this devised conditional faith that gives them title to Christ.[24] Seemingly, Marshall had Baxter in mind while writing this section. He even uses the same metaphor of "pepper corn" to show the fallacy of Neonomianism. He comments on the metaphor that pictures our evangelical righteousness as a pepper corn as follows: "And though it is accounted but as the payment of a peppercorn for a great estate, yet it is enough to break the ablest man in the world, because it debars him from laying hold of the only effectual means of holiness, by which that peppercorn may be obtained."[25] To sum up, while giving an exposition of the meaning of justification, Marshall describes the error of Neonomianism and the reason for their emergence in the following words:

> This is a great mystery (contrary to the apprehensions, not only of the vulgar, but of some learned divines) that we must be reconciled to God and justified by the remission of our sins and imputation of righteousness, before any sincere obedience to the law, that we may be enabled for the practice of it. They account that this doctrine tends to the subversion of a holy practice, and is a great pillar of Antinomianism, and that the only way to establish sincere obedience is to make it rather a condition to be performed before our actual justification and reconciliation with God. Therefore, some late divines have thought fit to bring the doctrine of former

---

22. Marshall, *Gospel Mystery of Sanctification*, 100–101.
23. Marshall, *Gospel Mystery of Sanctification*, 118.
24. Marshall, *Gospel Mystery of Sanctification*, 119.
25. Marshall, *Gospel Mystery of Sanctification*, 119.

Protestants concerning justification to their anvil, and to hammer it into another form, that it might be more free from Antinomianism and effectual to secure a holy practice. But their labour is vain and pernicious, tending to Antinomian profaneness, or painted hypocrisy at best.[26]

Therefore, "Neonomianism tried to keep people from falling into the cheap grace of Antinomianism, but they did so by placing people back under the law again."[27] In fact, Neonomianism fell in the same error of the Papists by confusing justification and sanctification. With respect to the relation between justification and sanctification, Marshall follows the teaching of the Puritans who denied the teaching of both the Antinomians and the Neonomians. Against the Antinomians, "they concur with Richard Baxter in the necessity for "Law-keeping" by the believer, but they also reject his Neonomianism."[28] As we will see, in Marshall's view, justification opens the way to sanctification, but it is not itself sanctification.

Distinct Yet Inseparable

Marshall is clear from the beginning of his book that holiness, which he calls spiritual universal obedience, is "the great end to the attainment of which he is directing us."[29] However, Marshall is keen to achieve this holiness through the powerful and effectual means of the gospel. He seeks to maintain a balance in which justification and sanctification are distinct yet inseparable. Marshall teaches that "holiness in this life is absolutely necessary to salvation, not only as a means to the end, but by a nobler kind of necessity, as part of the end itself. Though we are not saved by good works, as procuring causes, yet we are saved to good works, as fruits and effects of saving grace, which God has prepared that we should walk in them (Eph 2:10)."[30] For Marshall, we are not justified by obedience; however, justification can never be separated from obedience as a necessary consequence. Ernest Kevan affirms this idea by saying that "it was the common dictum of the Puritans that a godly life was the evidence of faith."[31] Marshall's view

26. Marshall, *Gospel Mystery of Sanctification*, 22.
27. McRae, "Introduction," 8.
28. Kevan, *Grace of Law*, 206.
29. Marshall, *Gospel Mystery of Sanctification*, 3.
30. Marshall, *Gospel Mystery of Sanctification*, 150.
31. Kevan, *Grace of Law*, 208.

is a representation of this teaching. For instance, he says, "A lively faith cannot be without fruits."[32] In another instance where Marshall speaks of the comforts of the gospel, he emphasizes the inseparability of justification and sanctification. For Marshall, the comforts of the gospel "are given before the sincere practice of the law, yet they are not given to us in our corrupt sinful nature, but in and with new holy nature, which immediately produces a holy practice."[33]

On the other hand, Marshall maintains a distinctiveness between justification and sanctification. "Justification signifies 'making just' while sanctification signifies 'making holy.'"[34] Marshall argues that "making just" is a judicial expression in which we are discharged from our guilt, freed from blame and accusation, and are pronounced righteous.[35] This righteousness that is imputed to us is "an everlasting righteousness by which our standing in Christ is secured . . . it is an effectual, *complete*, and perpetual redemption, reaching the conscience of the sinner, and for the purging away of all sins, present and to come (1 John 1:7)."[36] Conversely, For Marshall sanctification is not judicial; rather it is a conformity to God's law, a restoration of the image of God engraved upon man in the first creation. Moreover, Marshall asserts that the renewing process of sanctification is never perfect in this life and shall be perfected in our glorification.[37]

This concept of the distinctiveness and inseparability of justification and sanctification is not pioneered by Marshall. We find the same assertions in the writings of Calvin. In his refutation of Osiander's ideas, who erroneously mixed justification with regeneration, Calvin is careful to show that although distinct in meaning, justification and sanctification can never be separated in the Christian's life. Calvin teaches

> As Christ cannot be torn into parts, so these two which we perceive in him together and conjointly are inseparable—namely, righteousness and sanctification. . . . But if the brightness of the sun cannot be separated from its heat, shall we therefore say that the earth is warmed by its light, or lighted by its heat? Is there anything more applicable to the present matter than this comparison?

32. Marshall, *Gospel Mystery of Sanctification*, 139.
33. Marshall, *Gospel Mystery of Sanctification*, 156.
34. Marshall, "Doctrine of Justification Opened," 2.
35. Marshall, "Doctrine of Justification Opened," 2–3.
36. Marshall, "Doctrine of Justification Opened," 19–20. Italics are mine.
37. Marshall, *Gospel Mystery of Sanctification*, 3–4.

> The sun, by its heat, quickens and fructifies the earth, by its beams brightens and illumines it. Here is a mutual and indivisible connection. . . . Osiander mixes that gift of regeneration with this free acceptance and contends that they are one and the same. Yet Scripture, even though it joins them, still lists them separately in order that God's manifold grace may better appear to us. For Paul's statement is not redundant: that Christ was given to us for our righteousness and sanctification [1 Cor 1:30].[38]

Furthermore, Calvin teaches that justification is a completed fact while sanctification is a continuing process which is never perfect in this life. He explains justification as "the acceptance with which God receives us into his favor as righteous men. And we say that it consists in the remission of sins and the imputation of Christ's righteousness."[39] Accordingly, our condemnation is forever removed because our justification is accomplished.[40] With regard to sanctification, in his commentary on the Gospel of John, Calvin says, "We ought to infer from Christ's words, that *sanctification* is not instantly completed in us on the first day, but that we make progress in it through the whole course of our life."[41]

Not only Calvin, but also the Westminster Assembly retained a balance between the inseparability and distinctiveness of justification and sanctification. The Assembly was concerned to distinguish justification from sanctification (against Roman Catholicism), yet they wanted to keep justification and sanctification inseparable (against Antinomianism). A clear and direct explanation of the relation between justification and sanctification is shown in the *Westminster Larger Catechism*, question 77:

> Q. 77. Wherein do justification and sanctification differ?
> A. Although sanctification be inseparably joined with justification, yet they differ, in that God in justification imputeth the righteousness of Christ; in sanctification his Spirit infuseth grace, and enableth, to the exercise thereof; in the former sin is pardoned; in the other it is subdued: the one doth equally free all believers from the revenging wrath of God, and that perfectly in this life, that they never fall into condemnation the other is neither equal in all, nor in this life perfect in any, but growing up to perfection.

---

38. Calvin, *Inst.* 3.11.6.
39. Calvin, *Inst.* 3.11.2.
40. Calvin, *Inst.* 3.2.24.
41. Calvin, *Calvin's Commentaries*, John 17:17.

The Assembly emphasizes the same distinctiveness that Marshall makes. Justification and sanctification cannot be separated. In justification, judicial and relational aspects with God are highlighted, while in sanctification, a transformational aspect is highlighted. Finally, justification is perfect and equal in all believers, but sanctification differs from one believer to another and is imperfect throughout all of this life. The important principle that helps us to understand this balance between justification and sanctification as distinct yet inseparable is union with Christ.

Union with Christ

Union with Christ is central in Marshall's view of sanctification. For him, "this union is not the end but the beginning of the sanctified life."[42] As he argues against Neonomianism, Marshall refuses the claim that union with Christ relates only to justification: "They account that, though they be justified by a righteousness wrought out by Christ, yet they must be sanctified by a holiness wrought out by themselves."[43] Contrarily, Marshall asserts that both our justification and sanctification come to us only through our communion with Christ. He teaches that "as we are justified by a righteousness wrought out in Christ and imputed so we are sanctified by such a holy frame and qualifications as are first wrought out and completed in Christ for us, and then imparted to us."[44] Against any Neonomian claim that could see the Protestant teaching about justification as an excuse for Antinomianism, Marshall points to the inseparability of justification and sanctification rooted in union with Christ. He contends:

> This comfortable persuasion of our justification and future happiness and all saving privileges cannot tend to licentiousness, as it is given only in this way of union with Christ, because it is joined inseparably with the gift of sanctification, by the Spirit of Christ, so that we cannot have justification, or any saving privilege in Christ, except we receive Christ Himself and His holiness, as well as any other benefit; as the Scripture testifies that there is no condemnation to them that are in Christ Jesus, who walk not after the flesh, but after the Spirit (Rom 8:1).[45]

---

42. Wakefield, "Protestant Mysticism," 266.
43. Marshall, *Gospel Mystery of Sanctification*, 42.
44. Marshall, *Gospel Mystery of Sanctification*, 41.
45. Marshall, *Gospel Mystery of Sanctification*, 57.

Andrew Murray is helpful in explaining the centrality of the union with Christ in Marshall's theology. He comments, "the beauty of Marshall's book is that he makes union with Christ the starting-point in the Christian course. He points out how by faith the sinner receives Christ and His salvation; how *justification and sanctification* are both given in Christ, and received only through faith that unites with Him."[46] Joel Beeke in his introduction to Marshall's book comments on the inseparability of justification and sanctification in Marshall's thinking: "As it is essential to be united with Christ in justification, so is it essential that we know Him experientially in sanctification. The religion of Marshall and the Puritans was filled with vitality because it encompassed both."[47]

Once again, we find a strong resemblance in the theology of both Marshall and Calvin. Union with Christ was central to Calvin's theology. He argues that "we must understand that as long as Christ remains outside of us, and we are separated from him, all that he has suffered and done for the salvation of the human race remains useless and of no value for us."[48] Calvin faced accusations from the Papists that justification by faith alone downplayed the necessity of good works. This attack aimed for a legalistic religion and accused the Protestant doctrine of justification of leading to Antinomianism. In fact, this accusation is quite similar to what Marshall encountered from Neonomianism. To answer such an accusation, Calvin needed to show that what he teaches was against legalism and at the same time never leads to licentiousness. To achieve his aim, Calvin maintained the inseparable relation between justification and sanctification on the ground of our union with Christ. In his commentary on 1 Cor 1:30, Calvin refutes those false accusations: "Let therefore the man who seeks to be justified through Christ, by God's unmerited goodness, consider that this cannot be attained without his taking him at the same time for sanctification."[49] Moreover, he uses the same text in the *Institutes* to show the way that union with Christ is the ground for the inseparability of justification and sanctification:

> Since the question concerns only righteousness and sanctification, let us dwell upon these. Although we may distinguish them, Christ contains both of them inseparably in himself. Do you wish, then, to attain righteousness in Christ? You must first possess Christ;

---

46. Murray, "Introduction," 3. Italics are mine.
47. Beeke, "Introduction," xxi.
48. Calvin, *Inst.* 3.1.1.
49. Calvin, *Calvin's Commentaries*, 1 Cor 1:30.

but you cannot possess him without being made partaker in his sanctification, because he cannot be divided into pieces [1 Cor. 1:13]. Since, therefore, it is solely by expending himself that the Lord gives us these benefits to enjoy, he bestows both of them at the same time, the one never without the other. Thus it is clear how true it is that we are justified not without works yet not through works, since in our sharing in Christ, which justifies us, sanctification is just as much included as righteousness.[50]

Marshall's view here also resonates with the view of the Westminster Assembly which grounded the inseparability of justification and sanctification on union with Christ. Thomas Torrance claimed that "the Westminster Confession emphasizes that union with Christ is inseparable from sanctification but not from justification."[51] However, a closer look at the *Confession* shows that the divines made a strong connection between justification and effectual calling: "Those whom God effectually calls, he also freely justifies."[52] The effectual calling is God's grace to his elect by which he powerfully and graciously draws them to Christ by the Holy Spirit (10.1).[53] Therefore, God by his effectual gracious call draws his elect to Christ to be justified. Tudur Jones rightly argues that the Assembly saw the effectual calling as the means that actualizes our union with Christ.[54] Jones says, "The Westminster Assembly's Larger Catechism describes the union of the elect with Christ as the work of God's grace, which is done in their effectual calling. So union with Christ is contemporaneous with effectual calling and precedes Justification, Adoption and Sanctification."[55] Furthermore, the *Larger Catechism* asserts that the communion of the believer with Christ is the relation through which all the blessings of salvation flows to their lives, including justification and sanctification.

> Q. 69 What is the communion in grace which the members of the invisible church have with Christ?

---

50. Calvin, *Inst.* 3.16.1.
51. Torrance, *Scottish Theology*, 144.
52. *Westminster Confession of Faith* 11.1.
53. Letham, *Westminster Assembly*, 269.
54. *Westminster Larger Catechism*, question 66: "What is that union which the elect have with Christ? A. The union which the elect have with Christ is the work of God's grace, whereby they are spiritually and mystically, yet really and inseparably, joined to Christ as their head and husband; which is done in their effectual calling."
55. Tudur, "Union With Christ," 190.

A. The communion in grace which the members of the invisible church have with Christ, is their partaking of the virtue of his mediation, in their justification, adoption, sanctification, and whatever else, in this life, manifests their union with him.

Accordingly, and similarly to Marshall, the Westminster Assembly taught an inseparable relation between union with Christ and all the blessings of salvation, including justification and sanctification. In fact, the *Larger Catechism* shows that both justification and sanctification are inevitable results of union with Christ. J. V. Fesko comments on the teaching of the Assembly at this point by saying that

> the various elements found within the *Confession* (effectual calling, justification, adoption, sanctification, perseverance, and glorification) all manifest the believer's union with Christ. These different elements of salvation are not steps that progressively lead to union but are instead the constituent elements both of their union and of the unbreakable golden chain of salvation.[56]

Faith: Instrument for Double Grace

Marshall argues that union with Christ is foundational for both justification and sanctification. For Marshall, the means by which the Spirit of God accomplishes this union with Christ is faith. Faith is the instrument by which we receive Christ himself with all his fullness,[57] including our justification and sanctification. Marshall sees faith as believing in Christ, not only out of fear of damnation, but also "with a hearty love and desire towards the enjoyment of Him."[58] Then Marshall interprets this loving reception of Christ by faith as loving "every part of Christ's salvation—holiness a well as forgiveness of sins"[59]—justification and sanctification.

Marshall refuses any claim that attaches faith to justification but not to sanctification. He argues for the uniqueness of faith as the sole instrument for both justification and sanctification. Marshall's adversaries argue that, although justification is by faith, yet sanctification is by works; they think

---

56. Fesko, *Theology of the Westminster Standards*, 252.
57. Marshall, *Gospel Mystery of Sanctification*, 61.
58. Marshall, *Gospel Mystery of Sanctification*, 62.
59. Marshall, *Gospel Mystery of Sanctification*, 62.

that this would protect the church from Antinomianism. Marshall explains such claims and comments on them as follows:

> Some will allow that faith is the sole condition of our justification and the instrument to receive it, according to the doctrine maintained formerly by the Protestants against the Papists; but they account that it is not sufficient or effectual to sanctification, but that it rather tends to licentiousness, if it is not joined with some other means that may be powerful and effectual to secure a holy practice . . . their corrective antidote is that that sanctification is necessary to salvation, as well as justification; and though we are justified by faith, yet we are sanctified by our own performance of the law. So they set up salvation by works, and make the grace of justification to be of no effect, and not at all comfortable.[60]

From the previous quotation, we see that Marshall does not only refuse this dichotomy between sanctification and justification with respect to their relation to faith, but also argues that that dichotomy robs justification of its comforts and its importance for sanctification. Furthermore, this dichotomy would lead to the remodeling of the meaning of faith "to be only a condition to procure a right and title to our justification by the righteousness of Christ,"[61] instead of conceiving faith as the instrument by which we are united to Christ.[62]

Accordingly, Marshall holds to the inseparability between justification and sanctification in respect to their relation to faith. In his introduction to Marshall's book, Bruce McRae states that Walter Marshall emphasizes several ideas in order to keep the balance against both legalism and cheap grace. Among these ideas is that "if you have come to faith in Christ, you participate in two blessings: your sins have been forgiven, and you have received a new heart and a new nature through the filling of the Holy Spirit. You have become a 'new creation.'"[63] Marshall teaches clearly that "faith is an instrument by which we actually receive Christ Himself into our hearts, and holiness of heart and life, as well as justification, by union and fellowship with Him."[64] In another place, he elaborates: "We do indeed assert

---

60. Marshall, *Gospel Mystery of Sanctification*, 65.
61. Marshall, *Gospel Mystery of Sanctification*, 66.
62. For more discussion about the debate about the meaning of faith in Marshall's theology, return to the previous two chapters on justification and sanctification.
63. McRae, "Introduction," 9.
64. Marshall, *Gospel Mystery of Sanctification*, 67.

and profess that 'A true and lively faith in Christ is alone sufficient and effectual, through the grace of God, to receive Christ and all His fullness, so far as is necessary in this life, for our justification, sanctification and eternal salvation."[65] James Hervey wrote the following lines about the direct relation of faith to both justification and sanctification in Marshall's theology:

> As faith is such a persuasion of the heat, and such a reception of Christ, it assures the soul of salvation by its own act; antecedent to all reflection on its fruits or effects, on marks or evidences—It assures the soul of acquaintance from guilt, and reconciliation to God; of a title to the everlasting inheritance, and of grace sufficient for every case of need. By the exercise of this faith, and the enjoyment of these blessings, we are sanctified.[66]

Calvin held a similar view to Marshall about the way that faith relates to both justification and sanctification. Calvin explicitly states, "Faith embraces Christ, as offered to us by the Father, that is, he is offered not only for righteousness, forgiveness of sins, and peace, but also for sanctification."[67] On the other hand, the Westminster Standards differed somewhat from Marshall and Calvin at this point, at least in terms of clarity.

The Westminster Assembly uses explicit language to express the direct relation between faith and justification in the *Westminster Confession of Faith*. In the chapter on justification, the *Confession* states that "faith, thus receiving and resting on Christ and his righteousness, is the *alone instrument of justification*; yet is it not alone in the person justified, but is ever accompanied with all other saving graces, and is no dead faith, but works by love."[68] However, this explicit language is not used to express that relation between faith and sanctification in the Westminster Standards.

Nevertheless, in question 75 on sanctification, the *Larger Catechism* teaches that the saving graces needed for our renewal unto the image of God are "*stirred up, increased, and strengthened*, so that we more and more may die unto sin and rise unto newness of life."[69] The proof texts used for stirring up, increasing, and strengthening the saving graces that sanctify us are Jude 20, Heb 6:11–12, Eph 3:16–19, and Col 1:10–11. The first three texts explicitly refer to faith as the means for that growth. This use of proof

---

65. Marshall, *Gospel Mystery of Sanctification*, 267.
66. Hervey, "Recommendation Letter to the Publisher," 330.
67. Calvin, *Inst.* 3.2.8.
68. *Westminster Confession of Faith* 11.2. Italics are mine.
69. *Westminster Larger Catechism*, question 75. Italics are mine.

texts shows that the Assembly believed that faith is the instrument for sanctification as well. Thomas Ridgley (1667–1734), whose commentary on the *Larger Catechism* is "indisputably the best,"[70] points to the role of faith in our sanctification. In his commentary on question 75, Ridgley argues that faith is not only essential in the beginning of our Christian life in which we surrender ourselves to Christ, but rather "our sanctification consists in continuance of this surrender and dependence."[71] Accordingly, Ridgley believes that "our exercise of faith must be our constant work to walk with God and live to him."[72] In conclusion, he writes:

> There is a vast difference between recommending or practicing moral virtues, as agreeable to the nature of man, and the dictates of reason; and a person's being led in that way of holiness which our Savior has prescribed in the gospel. This takes its rise from a change of nature wrought in regeneration, is excited by gospel-motives, is encourage by promises of holy attainment, and *proceeds from the grace of faith*, without which all pretensions to holiness are vain and defective.[73]

Justification and Sanctification: Cause and Effect

Up to this point, we have seen that Walter Marshall's doctrines of justification, sanctification, their inseparability, their relation to union with Christ, and their relation to faith, greatly resembles the doctrines of John Calvin and the Westminster Assembly. However, Marshall goes further and deeper in the manner that these two graces relate to each other. Not only does Marshall maintain that they are inseparable and distinct, but he also stresses a direct relationship between justification and sanctification. For him, the relation between justification and sanctification is a relation in which the former goes before the latter, "as the cause before the effect."[74] He contends that "sanctification is an effect of justification, and flows from the same grace; and we trust for them both by the same faith, and for the latter in order to the former."[75]

70. Beeke and Pederson, *Meet the Puritans*, 502.
71. Ridgley, *Body of Divinity*, 3:154.
72. Ridgley, *Body of Divinity*, 3:160.
73. Ridgley, *Body of Divinity*, 3:164. Italics are mine.
74. Marshall, *Gospel Mystery of Sanctification*, 117.
75. Marshall, *Gospel Mystery of Sanctification*, 323.

The same relation between justification and sanctification can be deduced from the teachings of Calvin and the Westminster Assembly. However, Marshall explains this relation in a more explicit way. In his sermons on the book of Galatians, Calvin teaches that our peace of conscience, which results from remission of sins, is our foundation that assures us of the love of God and allows us to call Him our Father, and hence we seek to "draw nearer to God in conformity to His holy will."[76]

Regarding the Westminster Assembly, some divines pointed to the priority of justification over sanctification or to the "cause-effect" relationship between them. For instance, Anthony Burgess argued that justification and sanctification are conjoined together "so that although there be a priority of nature" for justification, yet they are together in time.[77] Samuel Rutherford, one of the Scottish commissioners to the Assembly, argued that "Justification and Sanctification ought not to bee[sic] separated, but both concurre[sic] to make us Saints; the one as the cause, the other as the unseparable effect."[78] The *Westminster Confession* teaches in chapter 12 on adoption that being justified means that we are made "partakers of the grace of adoption," with all the privileges pertaining to it.[79] We cannot receive the gifts of God and the inheritance of God's children unless we are first reconciled and accepted with him. Only then are we in "a favorable position with God to receive all the gifts of God's love for His own people,"[80] including sanctification.[81]

Nevertheless, Marshall remains clearer and more explicit in his teaching about the way that sanctification flows from justification. In the previous chapter on sanctification, we saw how Marshall refers to four necessary endowments that we must possess before we can practice true holiness. The main endowment was a new propensity or inclination of the heart to holiness. However, Marshall asserted that this propensity is a rational propensity that is "fitting for intelligent creatures, by which they are, by the conduct of reason prone and bent to approve and choose their duty

---

76. Calvin, *Sermons on Galatians*, Gal 2:17–20.
77. Burgess, *True Doctrine of Justification*, 172.
78. Rutherford, *Survey of the Spirituall Antichrist*, 155.
79. *Westminster Confession of Faith* 12.1.
80. Morecraft, *Authentic Christianity*, 2: 725.
81. For more evidences on how justification and sanctification are directly relates in the Westminster Standard, please return to chapter 3 on "Justification and Sanctification in the Westminster Standards."

and averse to the practice of sin."[82] Therefore, Marshall argues that being persuaded of our reconciliation with God is the rational reason that causes the change of our inclination, thus our proper obedience of God's law.

Guilt and Bondage

Marshall sees a direct connection on one hand, between being guilty and being in bondage to sin, and on the other hand between being justified and being in love with God and his commandments. For Marshall, in our natural state, we are guilty "even of Adam's first sin, and of the sinful depravation of our nature, and of all our own actual transgressions, and therefore we are by nature the children of wrath (Eph 2:3) and under the curse of God."[83] This sense of guilt is accompanied by an evil conscience, "which denounces the wrath of God against us for sin, and inclines us to abhor Him as our enemy."[84] Marshall describes this deadly process in the following words:

> I have often considered by what manner of working any sin could effectually destroy the whole image of God in the first Adam, and I conclude it was by working first an evil guilty conscience in him, by which he judged that the just God was against him and cursed him for that one sin. And this was enough to work a shameful nakedness by disorderly lusts, a turning his love wholly from God to the creature, and a desire to be hidden from the presence of God (Gen. 3 8, 10) which was a total destruction of the image of God's holiness.[85]

This evil conscience that is full of guilt, and that "considers God as an enemy whose justice is against us to our everlasting condemnation because of our sins,"[86] results in more hatred towards God. Hatred towards God means more bondage to sin, because holiness in its essence means love for God and his commandments. Therefore, this natural state with all its miseries of guilt and hatred towards God and his judgments necessarily results in the "increase of the dominion of sin and Satan in us, and works most mischievous effects in the soul against godliness, even to bring the soul to hate God and to wish there were no God, no heaven, no hell, so

82. Marshall, *Gospel Mystery of Sanctification*, 17.
83. Marshall, *Gospel Mystery of Sanctification*, 87.
84. Marshall, *Gospel Mystery of Sanctification*, 87.
85. Marshall, *Gospel Mystery of Sanctification*, 27–28.
86. Marshall, *Gospel Mystery of Sanctification*, 27.

we might escape the punishment due to us."⁸⁷ This endless cycle of guilt and hatred that Marshall describes, "makes spiritual obedience to the law impossible."⁸⁸ Humans can never prevail against sin while they are the children of wrath and cursed by God. Our evil conscience that is stained by our guilt will "itself be a cause of our committing more sin."⁸⁹ Instead of loving God and his commandments, "the soul will wish secretly that God was not, or that he were not so just a judge; which is a secret cursing of God."⁹⁰ Marshall concludes that this devastating cycle will eventually lead to the disaffection of people against God.

> They cannot endure to think, or speak, or hear of Him and His law, but strive rather to put Him out of their minds by fleshly pleasures and worldly employments. And thus they are alienated from all true religion, only binding it and stopping the mouth of it. It produces zeal in many outside religious performances, and also false religion, idolatry and the most inhuman superstitions in the world.⁹¹

Justification and Love

The concept of love is central to Marshall in the relation between justification and sanctification. As noted earlier in the chapter on sanctification, to be holy is to love God and his commandments. Contrarily, being guilty and under God's curse induces hatred towards God. Marshall argues that in our natural state of guilt and under God's wrath, we can never love God properly. For Marshall, our proper love to God is

> a love by which we like everything in Him as He is our Lord—His justice as well as any other attribute—without wishing or desiring that He were better than He is; and by which we desire that His will may be done on us and all others, whether prosperity or adversity, life or death; and by which we can heartily praise Him for all things, and delight in our obedience to Him, in doing His

---

87. Marshall, *Gospel Mystery of Sanctification*, 27.
88. Lee, "Sanctification by Faith," 82.
89. Marshall, *Gospel Mystery of Sanctification*, 26.
90. Marshall, *Gospel Mystery of Sanctification*, 28.
91. Marshall, *Gospel Mystery of Sanctification*, 27.

will, though we suffer that which is ever so grievous to us, even present death."[92]

Marshall contends that what motivates us to love God is not just his perfection and excellence. In fact, "the greater God's excellency and perfection is, the greater evil He is to us, if He hates and curses us,"[93] due to our guilt and sinfulness. Marshall further explains that "the principle of self-preservation, deeply rooted in our natures, hinders us from loving that which we apprehend as our destruction."[94]

Accordingly, this endless cycle of guilt, bondage to sin, curse from God, and hatred towards him will never be broken "except this guilt and curse be removed from us; which is done by actual justification,"[95] Marshall argues. Therefore, in order to be holy, that is to love God, "our conscience must of necessity be first purged from dead works."[96] For Marshall, the only way to have good conscience and void of offense towards God is through "the blood of Christ applied by faith which takes off the foulness of guilt from the conscience."[97] To be justified means that we enjoy reconciliation with God, remission of sins and cleansing of our consciences from dead works. Then, we can practice our duty to love God properly, as we apprehend his love and goodness toward us in justifying us from our sins and in imputing righteousness to us.[98]

Marshall gives many examples to argue for this relation between being reconciled with God and obeying him. Two of these examples are the first and the last Adams. For both, Adam and Christ, their obedience to God—that is their holiness—was tied to their loving relationship with God. Marshall argues that before the fall, "God gave to Adam, at his first creation, the comfort of His love and favour and the happiness of Paradise, to encourage him to obedience, and when he had lost these comforts by the Fall, he was no longer able to obey until he was restored by new comfort of the promised seed."[99] The same principle applies with Christ, the second Adam. Marshall goes on to say that "Christ, the second Adam, set God always

92. Marshall, *Gospel Mystery of Sanctification*, 25.
93. Marshall, *Gospel Mystery of Sanctification*, 26.
94. Marshall, *Gospel Mystery of Sanctification*, 26.
95. Marshall, *Gospel Mystery of Sanctification*, 24.
96. Marshall, *Gospel Mystery of Sanctification*, 26.
97. Marshall, "Doctrine of Justification Opened," 19.
98. Marshall, *Gospel Mystery of Sanctification*, 25.
99. Marshall, *Gospel Mystery of Sanctification*, 164.

before His face and He knew that, because God was at His right hand, He should not be moved; therefore, His heart was glad, and His glory rejoiced (Ps. 16:8, 9). This made Him willing to bear His agony and bloody sweat, and to be obedient to death, even the death of the cross."[100]

To conclude, Marshall believes that sanctification must flow from the comfort of justification. Joel Beeke argues that "Marshall's book teaches us that sanctification cannot increase in our lives and churches without the Word-centered teaching of gracious justification by faith."[101] The peace with God promised in the gospel and our holiness are tied together. For Marshall, "peace, joy and hope of the gospel are considered as the spring of our holy duties."[102] Marshall contends that no true holiness can exist without enjoying the comfort of the gospel which is granted through justification in Christ.

Antinomianism—Neonomianism—Antinomianism

In holding fast to his view of justification, sanctification and their relation, Marshall emphasizes gospel holiness against the errors of Antinomianism and Neonomianism. He asserts that "Christ will save none but those that are brought to resign themselves sincerely to the obedience of His royal authority and laws."[103] However, this obedience is not the means of reconciliation with God. In fact, this obedience becomes reality only by receiving salvation from God. Therefore, Marshall makes this clarification on the place of obedience in our spiritual life:

> The Ten Commandments bind us still, as they were then given to a people that were at that time under the covenant of grace made with Abraham, to show them what duties are holy, just and good, well-pleasing to God, and to be a rule for their conversation. The result of all is that we must still practice moral duties as commanded by Moses, but we must not seek to be justified by our practice.[104]

Clearly, Marshall holds to the inseparability between sanctification and justification against Antinomianism. Moreover, he holds to the idea

---

100. Marshall, *Gospel Mystery of Sanctification*, 164.
101. Beeke, "Introduction," xx.
102. Marshall, *Gospel Mystery of Sanctification*, 156.
103. Marshall, *Gospel Mystery of Sanctification*, 137.
104. Marshall, *Gospel Mystery of Sanctification*, 109.

that "we must be reconciled to God and justified by the remission of our sins and imputation of righteousness, before any sincere obedience to the law."[105] Marshall understands that on the other extreme and out of fear of Antinomianism, Neonomianism wants to establish sincere obedience (sanctification) as a condition to be performed before our actual justification and reconciliation with God.[106] Neonomianism teaches that "the effectual way to secure the obedience we owe to the law of God is to ground all our comforts on the performance of it."[107] That error Marshall also rejected.

Marshall describes that the Neonomian doctrine that puts sincere obedience as the condition of salvation as a relapse to legalism. He goes on to say, "It requires of us the performance of sincere obedience, before we have the means necessary to produce it, by making it antecedent to our justification, and persuasion of eternal happiness, and our actual enjoyment of union and fellowship with Christ, and of that new nature which is to be had only in Him by faith."[108] Marshall argues that this way is in itself "destructive to the means of holiness and to holiness itself."[109]

For Marshall, although Neonomianism claims that it promotes holiness and obedience, but in fact it does the contrary. Adam Gib in his recommendation to Marshall's book says that "adherence to a legal scheme of holiness vainly makes it the reason of their peace and hope."[110] Placing our reconciliation with God as a result of our holiness would lead to slavish obedience out of fear. Marshall argues that this labor is "vain and pernicious, tending to Antinomian profaneness, or painted hypocrisy at best."[111] He contends that failure to perform the condition of obedience results in anger and more hatred against the law and against God.[112] In our natural state, the inevitable effect of legal doctrine on our carnal heart is despair. Then, more hatred to God rises as we expect to be damned eternally for this disobedience. Consequently, the result is total abandonment of all religion and disobedience of the law. Therefore, Marshall argues that

---

105. Marshall, *Gospel Mystery of Sanctification*, 22.
106. Marshall, *Gospel Mystery of Sanctification*, 22.
107. Marshall, *Gospel Mystery of Sanctification*, 155.
108. Marshall, *Gospel Mystery of Sanctification*, 118.
109. Marshall, *Gospel Mystery of Sanctification*, 118.
110. Gib, "Recommendation by the Reverend Mr Adam Gib," vii.
111. Marshall, *Gospel Mystery of Sanctification*, 22.
112. Marshall, *Gospel Mystery of Sanctification*, 126.

Neonomianism is in fact the worst Antinomian error. He explains this idea in the following words:

> This is the pestilent effect of legal doctrine upon a carnal heart, that does but rouse up and terribly enrage the sleeping lion, our sinful corruption, instead of killing it—as is too evident by the sad experience of many that have endeavoured with all their might to practice it, and by the Scripture, that shows a sufficient cause why it cannot be otherwise. Therefore, the doctrine of salvation by sincere obedience, that was invented against Antinomianism, may well be ranked among the worst Antinomian errors. For my part, I hate it with perfect hatred, and account it mine enemy, as I have found it to be. And I have found by some good experience the truth of the lesson taught by the apostle, that the way to be freed from the mastery and dominion of sin is not to be under the law, but under grace (Rom 6:14).[113]

In this quotation, we see that Marshall himself suffered from this doctrine. As Skevington says, "*The Gospel Mystery of Sanctification* was spun out of Marshall's own experience."[114] McRae describes Marshall's struggle: "His religion only caused him affliction and heartache. He had been very distressed about the state of his soul for many years and he had tried to put his sins to death with many different methods. He had tried to gain peace of conscience by his own efforts but his mental anguish only increased."[115] This struggle remains until a life-changing encounter happened when he consulted Thomas Goodwin, whose words were "the turning point in Marshall's spiritual pilgrimage."[116] Goodwin told Marshall that "he had forgotten to mention the greatest sin of all, the sin of unbelief in not believing on the Lord Jesus for the remission of his sins and sanctifying his nature."[117] This reply showed Marshall his mistake that "he had all unconsciously been striving to establish his own righteousness and had not submitted himself to the righteousness of God."[118]

Accordingly, Marshall believes that the doctrine of salvation by sincere obedience is in contradiction to salvation by the gospel. For Marshall,

---

113. Marshall, *Gospel Mystery of Sanctification*, 126–27.
114. Wood, "Walter Marshall," 21.
115. McRae, "Introduction," 10.
116. Wood, "Walter Marshall," 22.
117. N., "Preface."
118. Wood, "Walter Marshall," 22.

when we are justified and reconciled with God, then "everlasting life has begun in us already."[119] As a result of this everlasting life, our holy practice begins. Marshall adds, "Therefore the beginning of everlasting life in us must not be placed after such a practice, as the fruit and consequence of it; but must go before it, as the cause before the effect."[120] Justification and sanctification are never inseparable in Marshall's thinking but they must follow this certain order, in which sanctification flows from justification. James Hervey commends Marshall's theology as he says,

> Here I apprehend, our Author will appear singular, this is the place in which he seems to go quite out of the common road. The generality of serious people look upon these unspeakable blessings as the reward of holiness; to be received, after we have sincerely practiced universal holiness. This is the stumbling-block, which our legal minds, dim with prejudice, and swollen with pride, will hardly get over. However, these endowments (among which justification is) of our new state are, in our Author's opinion, the effectual, and the only effectual expedient to produce sanctification.[121]

Conclusion

As we have seen, Marshall insists that justification and sanctification are distinct, inseparable, and orderly. In union with Christ we have the two graces of justification and sanctification. Beeke states that "union with Christ in our status before God (i.e., justification) must bring us closer to Christ in daily living (i.e., sanctification)."[122] Marshall also asserts that sanctification must flow from justification. He completely rejects any notion that exchanges that order. Mcrae comments on Marshall's teachings: "The gospel says that through faith in Christ, you are completely forgiven of all your sins. Then having been forgiven, you are called to sanctification by faith in Christ as well."[123] For Marshall the result in reversing that order is ungodliness. Legalism is the greatest Antinomian error. Only the persuasion of the love of God results in holiness, and the lack of persuasion of that

---

119. Marshall, *Gospel Mystery of Sanctification*, 117.
120. Marshall, *Gospel Mystery of Sanctification*, 117.
121. Hervey, "Recommendation Letter to the Publisher," 330–31.
122. Beeke, "Introduction," xx.
123. McRae, "Introduction," 6.

love leads to licentiousness.[124] This love of God for us is best manifested in Christ's death to save us from our sins. Marshall concludes:

> He made us first partakers of salvation, and that we shall never obey Him as a Lawgiver, until we receive Him as a Savior. He is a saving Lord; trust on Him first to save you from the guilt and power of sin, and dominion of Satan, and to give you a new spiritual disposition; then, and not till then, the love of Christ will constrain you to resign yourself heartily to live to Him that died for you (2 Cor. 5:14).[125]

---

124. Marshall, *Gospel Mystery of Sanctification*, 22–23.
125. Marshall, *Gospel Mystery of Sanctification*, 138.

Conclusion and Prospect

Dr. C. John Miller has been reported to say that "Dr. John Murray, late professor of systematic theology at Westminster Seminary in Philadelphia, had told him that Marshall's book *The Gospel Mystery of Sanctification* was the most important book on sanctification that had ever been written."[1] In that book, Marshall answered the questions "How do Christians become holy?" and "Where does the power for godly living come from?" Although the book answered these questions from different angles, this book was more concerned with the way Marshall explained the relation between justification and sanctification to achieve his aim, with the doctrine of the union with Christ in view. Moreover, the book investigated the way Marshall addressed the two dangerous errors of Antinomianism and Neonomianism that are directly related to these doctrines. For a better understanding of Marshall's views, his teachings were prefaced by John Calvin's view about the relation between justification and sanctification; as well as the Westminster Assembly's teachings upon the same subjects.

John Calvin asserted that justification and sanctification are distinct yet inseparable. This relation is guarded by the virtue of our union with Christ, through which these two graces flow. Regarding the Westminster Assembly, "the divines were equally concerned about the twofold benefit of union with Christ: justification and sanctification."[2] The divines gave a "nuanced exposition of the Protestant understanding of justification of faith alone through Christ alone,"[3] to avoid the two dangers of Antinomianism and legalism. They did so by holding to the distinct, inseparable, logically arranged relationship of justification and sanctification. However, the

---

1. McRae, "Introduction," 5.
2. Fesko, *Theology of the Westminster Standards*, 266.
3. Keller, "Foreword," 12.

problem of law and of obedience in the Christian life remained a pressing one. Though the Reformers and the Puritans held to the doctrine of justification by faith alone, the place of the law continues to be a subject of great debates and controversies. Ernest Kevan rightly expressed the struggle to understand the place of the law in the life of the church: "Throughout the centuries of Christianity, it has been recognized by the wisest and deepest thinkers that the right holding together of the requirements of the Law and the liberty of the Spirit is one of the harder tasks in theology."[4] The worldwide church overall up to this day still has to face this struggle while holding to the gospel of Christ. Marshall's contribution was a great help to the church in his time to face that struggle, and it still can be of a great help to the church today as it faces the same challenge.

Three Applications

We can learn many lessons from Marshall's book. However, we will highlight three main applications that can be learned from his view of the relation between justification and sanctification.

The Gospel Is the Remedy

Marshall's opposition against legalism and Antinomianism was one fight. Both errors are strongly connected. In fact, we are prone to swing between these two errors. Each of them leads to the other. When we think that being forgiven in Christ means that we are not bound to the law, we fall into Antinomianism. As a reaction against Antinomianism, we can go to the other extreme, which is legalism. In legalism, we try to secure obedience by making it the condition for our salvation and hence it becomes a heavy burden. Marshall was very aware of these two errors and the way that we are prone to swing between them. He argued that both errors reap one result, which is ungodliness.

> What a lamentable disappointment is this to those that have attempted to alter the Protestant doctrine, and to pervert and confound law and gospel, and have bred much contention in the church, that they might secure the practice of sincere obedience against Antinomian errors, by making it the procuring condition

---

4. Kevan, *Grace of Law*, 207.

of their salvation, when, after all this ado, the remedy is found to be as bad as the disease, equally unserviceable and destructive to that great end for which they designed it, and that it has an Antinomian effect and operation, contrary to the power of godliness!⁵

The final result of this swinging is despair, which leads to hatred of the law and subsequently of God. Marshall argues that "those who reach this horrible condition will end in either searing their consciences past feeling of sin and fully abandon all religion . . . or if they cannot sear their consciences, some of them are easily prevailed with by Satan, rather to murder themselves than to live longer in hatred to God."⁶ Sinclair Ferguson comments on this duality of legalism and Antinomianism: "Legalism and Antinomianism are, in fact, nonidentical twins that emerge from the same womb."⁷ Both of these errors participate in their hatred of obedience to God. Although legalism apparently promotes obedience, yet it is a burdensome obedience without joy. On the other hand, "Antinomianism refuses obedience too by claiming that if God is really loving, He wouldn't ask for it."⁸ Both errors stem from one root: distrust of God's goodness and graciousness.

The swinging between these two errors can only be broken by the gospel. Marshall argues that the only remedy of this horrible condition is the power of the gospel. In the gospel, we are assured of God's love for us manifested in the giving of Christ for us, through whose life, death, and resurrection, we are reconciled to God. Marshall's view of the gospel as the real remedy is resonated by Sinclair Ferguson:

> There is only one genuine cure for legalism. It is the same medicine the gospel prescribes for Antinomianism: understanding and tasting union with Jesus Christ himself. This leads to a new love for and obedience to the law of God, which he now mediates to us in the gospel. This alone breaks the bonds of both legalism (the law is no longer divorced from the person of Christ) and Antinomianism (we are not divorced from the law, which now comes to us from the hand of Christ and in the empowerment of the Spirit, who writes it in our hearts).⁹

---

5. Marshall, *Gospel Mystery of Sanctification*, 115–16.
6. Marshall, *Gospel Mystery of Sanctification*, 126.
7. Ferguson, *Whole Christ*, 84.
8. Keller, "Foreword," 14.
9. Ferguson, *Whole Christ*, 157.

The Right Use of the Law

The relation of believers to the law is at the heart of the fight against legalism and Antinomianism. If we say that we should not talk about obedience to the law, we move easily to Antinomianism. On the other hand, if we just use the language of threatening to make people obey the law, rather than seeing it as a gift from God, then we slip into legalism. Marshall argued that Christ is both a savior and a lawgiver. However, Marshall asserted that "we shall never obey Him as a lawgiver, until we receive Him as a Savior."[10]

Therefore, Marshall argued that the moral law represented in the Ten Commandments given to Moses does not bind us as a condition for justification.[11] Yet, this moral law still binds us, and we must practice its commandments as a rule of life of those who seek to please God out of love. For Marshall, "if we use the moral law as a rule of life, not as a condition of justification, it can be no ministration of death, or killing letter to us."[12] On the contrary, this moral law is "the most complete, excellently composed, and ordered by the wisdom of God and hence should be the rule of our lives as believers."[13]

We can find similar references to the proper use of the law in the life of the believers in the teachings of both John Calvin and the Westminster Assembly. Calvin defined three uses of the law. The first use is to show us our inability to fulfill it and thus lead us to seek grace in Christ.[14] The second use is to deter those who are unregenerate and to protect the community of saints.[15] Then the third use which Calvin calls the principal use, "finds its place among believers in whose hearts the Spirit of God already lives and reigns."[16] Calvin refused any notion of casting out the whole Mosaic law. He argued against those who try to abandon the two Tables of the law:

> Banish this wicked thought from our minds! For Moses has admirably taught that the law, which among sinners can engender nothing but death, ought among the saints to have a better and more excellent use.... But if no one can deny that a perfect pattern

---

10. Marshall, *Gospel Mystery of Sanctification*, 138.
11. Marshall, *Gospel Mystery of Sanctification*, 108.
12. Marshall, *Gospel Mystery of Sanctification*, 109.
13. Marshall, *Gospel Mystery of Sanctification*, 109.
14. Calvin, *Inst.* 2.7.1–9.
15. Calvin, *Inst.* 2.7.10–11.
16. Calvin, *Inst.* 3.7.12.

of righteousness stands forth in the law, either we need no rule to live rightly and justly, or it is forbidden to depart from the law.[17]

The *Westminster Confession of Faith* includes even more resemblance with Marshall in terms of Calvin's third use of the law. The *Confession* (19.6) teaches "the three great uses which apply to the moral law only,"[18] which are similar to Calvin's. In the first part of that paragraph the *Confession* begins with the Calvin's third use of the law: "Although true believers be not under the law, as a covenant of works, to be thereby justified, or condemned; yet is it of great use to them, as well as to others; in that, as a rule of life informing them of the will of God, and their duty, it directs and binds them to walk accordingly."[19] The *Confession* then goes on teach the other two uses of the law in the remainder of the paragraph.

Walter Marshall also held to the same three uses of the law that both Calvin and the Westminster Assembly taught. By the end of direction six of his book, Marshall stated these three uses of the law and applied them to the giving of the law to Moses. Of the first use of the law, he said the covenant of the law was added that "they might see their sinfulness and subjection to death and wrath, and the impossibility of attaining to life or holiness by their works, and be forced to trust on the free promise only for all their salvation."[20] Of the second use, Marshall taught that the law was given that "sin might be restrained by the spirit of bondage until the coming of that promised seed Jesus Christ, and the more plentiful pouring out of the sanctifying Spirit, by Him."[21] Finally, of the third use of the law, Marshall asserted that "the law was not given that any should ever attain to holiness or salvation by the condition of perfect or sincere obedience to it, though, if there had been any such way of salvation at that time, it must have consisted in the performance of that law, which was then given to the church to be a rule of life, as well as a covenant."[22] To conclude, Marshall emphasized that God's moral law still guides the life of the believers and can only be fulfilled in love by the power of the Spirit.

---

17. Calvin, *Inst.* 2.7.13.
18. Van Dixhoorn, *Confessing the Faith*, 250.
19. *Westminster Confession of Faith* 19.6.
20. Marshall, *Gospel Mystery of Sanctification*, 129.
21. Marshall, *Gospel Mystery of Sanctification*, 129.
22. Marshall, *Gospel Mystery of Sanctification*, 128.

Sufficiency of Christ

The third application is that we trust in Christ as sufficient for both our justification and sanctification. This application is relevant to countermand what is called the "second blessing" teaching. John Marshall comments on the second blessing teaching as "often associated with, at best an inadequate view of the law and at worse, with a scornful hostility to it."[23] In summary this idea teaches that sometimes when the gospel is preached, people may be converted and become Christians; yet "their experience does not correspond with the picture of the believer given in Scripture."[24] Therefore, this teaching claims that these people need a second blessing or a further experience that would allow them to live a better Christian life. However, the reality is that these so-called converted people are "mistakenly thinking they have become Christians when they really have no saving knowledge of Christ."[25] Marshall warned against such a dichotomy between believing in Christ for justification and for sanctification. He said, "When any fail in the second act of faith, the reason of the failing is commonly some defect in this first act.... If they knew the name of Christ, as He is discovered in the gospel, and judged aright of the truth and excellency of it, they would not fail to put their trust in Him."[26]

Contrary to the second-blessing teaching, Marshall argues for the sufficiency of Christ. In the books of Galatians and Colossians, we see attempts to add certain things to Christ's work in order to attain holiness and salvation. In Galatians, the Judaizers wanted to place Christians back under the requirements of the Mosaic law; while in Colossians, a higher life of mysticism is promoted as a complementary element.[27] The second blessing teaching claims that although we may be justified by faith, renewed by the Spirit, united with Christ, yet a second blessing is needed in order to live a holy life. Marshall joins the apostle Paul to reject such claims. Holiness comes from union with Christ, Marshall argues. As John Marshall argues, "Walter Marshall does not proceed by promoting dissatisfaction but

---

23. Marshall, "Walter Marshall and the Origins of Sanctification," 36.
24. Marshall, "Walter Marshall and the Origins of Sanctification," 36.
25. Beeke, "Introduction," xxiv.
26. Marshall, *Gospel Mystery of Sanctification*, 206.
27. McRae, "Introduction," 6.

Conclusion and Prospect

satisfaction—satisfaction with Christ and satisfaction in Christ."[28] Thus, we will conclude with this quotation from Marshall:

> You are to believe assuredly that there is no way to be saved without receiving all the saving benefits of Christ: His Spirit as well as His merits, sanctification as well as remission of sins, by faith. . . . You are to be fully persuaded of the all-sufficiency of Christ for the salvation of yourself, and of all that believe on Him; that His blood cleanses from all sin (1 John 1:7).[29]

---

28. Marshall, "Walter Marshall and the Origins of Sanctification," 38.
29. Marshall, *Gospel Mystery of Sanctification*, 208–9.

Bibliography

Allison, Gregg R. *Historical Theology: An Introduction to Christian Doctrine.* Grand Rapids, MI: Zondervan, 2011.
Arminius, Jacobus. *The Works of James Arminius,* Vol. 2. Translated by James Nichols and William Nichols. 3 vols. London ed. Grand Rapids, MI: Baker, 1996.
Baxter, Richard. *Aphorismes of Justification with Their Explication Annexed.* London: Tyton, 1649.
Beeke, Joel R. "Introduction." In *The Gospel Mystery of Sanctification,* by Walter Marshall, v–xxv. Grand Rapids, MI: Reformation Heritage, 1999.
———. *Living For God's Glory: An Introduction to Calvinism.* Lake Mary, FL: Reformation Trust, 2008.
Beeke, Joel R., and Mark Jones. *A Puritan Theology: Doctrine for Life.* Grand Rapids, MI: Reformation Heritage, 2012.
Beeke, Joel R., and Randall J. Pederson. *Meet the Puritans: With a Guide to Modern Reprints.* Grand Rapids, MI: Reformation Heritage, 2006.
Boersma, Hans. *A Hot Pepper Corn: Richard Baxter's Doctrine of Justification in its Seventeenth-Century Context of Controversy.* Zoetermeer: Uitgeverij Boekencentrum, 1993.
Bower, John. *The Larger Catechism: A Critical Text and Introduction.* Principle Documents of the Westminster Assembly. Grand Rapids, MI: Reformation Heritage, 2010.
Brooks, Thomas. *The Works of Thomas Brooks,* Vol. 5. Edited by Alexander Balloch Grosart. 6 vols. Edinburgh: Nichol, 1867.
Burgess, Anthony. *The True Doctrine of Justification: Asserted, and Vindicated, From The Errors of Papists, Arminians, Socinians, and More Especially Antinomians: in XXX Lectures Preached at Lawrence-Jury, London.* London: White, 1648.
Calvin, Jean. *Calvin's Commentaries.* 22 vols. Grand Rapids, MI: Baker, 1996.
———. *Institutes of The Christian Religion.* The Library of Christian Classics 20–21. Philadelphia: Westminster, 1960.
———. *Sermons on Galatians.* Edinburgh: Banner of Truth Trust, 1997.
Cameron, Andrew J. B. "How 'Ethics' Works: An Engagement with John Calvin." In *Engaging with Calvin: Aspects of The Reformer's Legacy for Today,* edited by Mark D. Thompson, 230–53. Nottingham: Apollos, 2009.
Christ, Mike. "A New Creation in Christ: A Historical-Theological Investigation into Walter Marshall's Theology of Sanctification in Union with Christ in the Context of the 17th-century Antinomian/Neonomian Controversy." PhD diss., University of Chester, 2016.

Bibliography

Edgar, William. "Ethics: The Christian Life and Good Works According to Calvin." In *A Theological Guide to Calvin's Institutes: Essays and Analysis*, edited by David W. Hall and Peter A. Lillback, 320–46. Calvin 500. Philipsburg, NJ: P & R, 2008.

Erskine, Ebenezer, et al. "Recommendatory Preface to the Edinburgh Edition 1733." In *The Gospel Mystery of Sanctification*, by Walter Marshall, v–vi. Edinburgh: Ogle, Doig & Stirling, and Whyte, 1815.

Ferguson, Sinclair B. "The Reformed View." In *Christian Spirituality: Five Views of Sanctification*, edited by Donald L. Alexander, 47–76. Downers Grove, IL: InterVarsity, 1988.

———. *The Whole Christ: Legalism, Antinomianism, and Gospel Assurance: Why the Marrow Controversy Still Matters*. Wheaton, IL: Crossway, 2016.

Fesko, J. V. *Beyond Calvin: Union with Christ and Justification in Early Modern Reformed Theology (1517–1700)*. Reformed Historical Theology 20. Göttingen: Vandenhoeck & Ruprecht, 2012.

———. *The Theology of the Westminster Standards: Historical Context and Theological Insights*. Wheaton, IL: Crossway, 2014.

Fisher, James, and Ebenezer Erskine. *The Westminster Assembly's Shorter Catechism Explained: By Way of Question and Answer*. Philadelphia: Presbyterian Board of Publication, 1850.

Flavel, John. *The Fountain of Life Opened, or, a Display of Christ in his Essential and Mediatorial Glory*. London: Tyton, 1673.

———. *The Method of Grace, in Bringing Home the Eternal Redemption Contrived by the Father, and Accomplished by the Son through the Effectual Application of the Spirit unto God's Elect, being the Second Part of Gospel Redemption*. London: Tyton, 1681.

Garcia, Mark A. *Life in Christ: Union With Christ and Twofold Grace in Calvin's Theology*. Studies in Christian History and Thought. Colorado Springs, CO: Paternoster, 2008.

Gerstner, John H. "The Nature of Justifying Faith." In *Justification by Faith Alone: Affirming the Doctrine by Which the Church and the Individual Stands or Falls*, edited by Don Kistler, 106–22. Morgan, PA: Soli Deo Gloria, 1995.

Gib, Adam. "A Recommendation by the Reverend Mr Adam Gib, Minister of the Gospel in the Associate Congregation of Edinburgh." In *The Gospel Mystery of Sanctification*, by Walter Marshall, vii. Edinburgh: Ogle, Doig & Stirling, and Whyte, 1815.

Gleason, Randall C. *John Calvin and John Owen on Mortification: A Comparative Study in Reformed Spirituality*. Studies in Church History vol. 3. New York: P. Lang, 1995.

Goodwin, Thomas. "The Object and Acts of Justifying Faith." In *The Works of Thomas Goodwin: Containing the Object and Acts of Justifying Faith*, 8:257–593. Edinburgh: Nichol, 1861.

Gwin, Timothy Joseph. "Mind and Heart Aflame: The Pilgrim Piety of John Calvin." Masters thesis, Reformed Theological Seminary, 2011.

Hawkes, Thomas Devonshire. "Pious Pastors: Calvin's Theology of Sanctification and How It Shaped The Teaching and Practices of The Genevan Academy, 1559–1564." PhD diss., Middlesex University, London School of Theology, 2013.

Helm, Paul. *John Calvin's Ideas*. Oxford: Oxford University Press, 2006.

Hervey, James. "Letter CIV on Marshall on Sanctification." In *The Works of James Hervey: Late Rector of Weston Favell, in Northamptonshire*, 5:333–36. London: Rivington, 1797.

Bibliography

———. "A Recommendatory Letter to the Publisher of a New Edition of Marshall on Sanctification." In *The Works of James Hervey: Late Rector of Weston Favell, in Northamptonshire*, 4:327–32. London: Rivington, 1797.

Hodge, Archibald Alexander, and J. Aspinwall Hodge. *The System of Theology Contained in the Westminster Shorter Catechism Opened and Explained*. Eugene, OR: Wipf & Stock, 2004.

Hoekema, Anthony A. *Created in God's Image*. Grand Rapids, MI: Eerdmans, 1986.

Keller, Timothy J. "Foreword." In *The Whole Christ: Legalism, Antinomianism, and Gospel Assurance: Why the Marrow Controversy Still Matters*, by Sinclair B. Ferguson, 11–16. Wheaton, IL: Crossway, 2016.

Kevan, Ernest F. *The Grace of Law: A Study in Puritan Theology*. London: Kingsgate, 1964.

Lee, Cheul Hee. "Sanctification by Faith: Walter Marshall's Doctrine of Sanctification in Comparison with the Keswick View of Sanctification." PhD diss., Pennsylvania, Westminster Theological Seminary, 2005.

Letham, Robert. *The Westminster Assembly: Reading Its Theology in Historical Context*. The Westminster Assembly and the Reformed Faith. Philipsburg, NJ: P & R, 2009.

Manton, Thomas. *The Complete Works of Thomas Manton*. Vol. 16, *Containing Sermons on Several Texts of Scripture*. 22 vols. London: Nisbet, 1870.

Marshall, John E. "Walter Marshall and the Origins of Sanctification." In *Aspects of Sanctification*, 17–40. Mirfield: The Westminster Conference, 1981.

Marshall, Walter. "The Doctrine of Justification Opened and Applied." In *The Gosper Mystery of Sanctification*. London: The Bible and Three Crowns, 1692.

———. *The Gospel Mystery of Sanctification: Opened in Sundry Practical Directions, Suited Especially to the Case of Those Who Labor under the Guilt and Power of Indwelling Sin, to which is added a Sermon of Justification*. London: The Bible and Three Crowns, 1692.

———. *Sanctification, or, The Highway of Holiness: an Abridgement (in the Author's Own Words) of the Gospel Mystery of Sanctification*. London: Nisbet, 1884.

McRae, Bruce H. "Introduction." In *Gospel Mystery of Sanctification: Growing in Holiness by Living in Union with Christ*, by Walter Marshall, 5–13. Eugene, OR: Wipf & Stock, 2005.

Morecraft, Joseph C. *Authentic Christianity: An Exposition of the Theology and Ethics of the Westminster Larger Catechism*. 5 vols. Powder Springs, GA: American Vision in cooperation with Minkoff Family, 2009.

Morris, Edward D. *Theology of the Westminster Symbols: A Commentary Historical, Doctrinal, Practical, on the Confession of Faith and Catechisms and the Related Formularies of the Presbyterian Churches*. Columbus, OH: Champlin, 1900.

Murray, Andrew. "Introduction." In *Sanctification, or, The Highway of Holiness, an Abridgement of the Gospel Mystery of Sanctification*, by Walter Marshall, 1–7. London: Nisbet, 1884.

N., N. "The Preface." In *The Gospel Mystery of Sanctification: Opened in Sundry Practical Directions, Suited Especially to the Case of Those Who Labor under the Guilt and Power of Indwelling Sin, to Which Is Added a Sermon of Justification*, by Walter Marshall, n.p. London: The Bible and Three Crowns, 1692.

Ngun, Richard. "A Survey of the Role of the Law in Sanctification among Selected Calvinists." *Stulos Theological Journal* 8.1–2 (2000) 45–71.

Owen, John. *An Exposition of the Epistle to the Hebrews with the Preliminary Exercitations*, Vol. 2. 4 vols. London: Pitcher, 1790.

———. *The Works of John Owen*. Vol. 3, *The Holy Spirit*. Edited by William H. Goold. 23 vols. London: Banner of Truth Trust, 1965.

Packer, James I. "'Keswick' and the Reformed Doctrine of Sanctification." *The Evangelical Quarterly* 27.3 (July 1955) 153–67.

———. *The Redemption & Restoration of Man in the Thought of Richard Baxter: A Study in Puritan Theology*. Vancouver, BC: Regent College, 2003.

Partee, Charles. *The Theology of John Calvin*. 1st ed. Louisville, KY: Westminster John Knox, 2008.

Pohl, Bert. "A Study of How the Gospel Is Effective Unto the Sanctification of the Believer." Masters thesis, Puritan Reformed Theological Seminary, 2005.

Ridgley, Thomas. *A Body of Divinity: Wherein the Doctrines of the Christian Religion are Explained and Defended, Being the Substance of Several Lectures on the Assembly's Larger Catechism*. Vol. 3. 4 vols. 1st American ed. Philadelphia: Woodward, 1814.

Rutherford, Samuel. *A Survey of the Spirituall Antichrist*. London: Crooke, 1648.

"The Savoy Declaration (1658)." https://www.creeds.net/congregational/savoy/.

Schroeder, Henry Joseph, ed. *Canons and Decrees of the Council of Trent*. St. Louis, MO: Herder, 1941.

Shaw, Robert. *The Reformed Faith: Exposition of the Westminster Confession of Faith*. Fearn, Scotland: Christian Focus, 2008.

Torrance, Thomas F. *Scottish Theology: from John Knox to John McLeod Campbell*. Edinburgh: T. & T. Clark, 1996.

Tudur, Jones R. "Union With Christ: The Existential Nerve of Puritan Piety." *Tudur Bulletin* 41.2 (1990) 186–208.

Van Dixhoorn, Chad B. *Confessing the Faith: A Reader's Guide to the Westminster Confession of Faith*. Edinburgh, Scotland: Banner of Truth Trust, 2014.

———. "The Strange Silence of Prolocutor Twisse: Predestination and Politics in the Westminster Assembly's Debate over Justification." *The Sixteenth Century Journal* 40.2 (2009) 395–418.

Van Dixhoorn, Chad B., et al., eds. *The Minutes and Papers of The Westminster Assembly, 1643–1652*. 5 vols. Oxford: Oxford University Press, 2012.

Wakefield, Gordon S. "Protestant Mysticism." *Preacher's Quarterly* 1.3 (1955) 264–68.

Watson, Thomas. *A Body of Divinity: Contained in Sermons Upon the Westminster Assembly's Catechism*. Edinburgh: Banner of Truth Trust, 2000.

Whyte, Alexander. "An Appreciation of Walter Marshall: The Most Pauline of Divines." In *The Apostle Paul*, 225–31. Minister's Paperback Library. Grand Rapids, MI: Baker, 1977.

Williamson, G. I. *The Westminster Confession of Faith for Study Classes*. 2nd ed. Philipsburg, NJ: P & R, 2004.

Wood, Arthur Skevington. "Walter Marshall and 'The Gospel Mystery of Sanctification.'" *The Evangelical Quarterly* 30.1 (1958) 18–29.

Wright, William A. *Calvin's Salvation in Writing: A Confessional Academic Theology*. Studies in Reformed Theology. Leiden: Brill, 2015.

www.ingramcontent.com/pod-product-compliance
Lightning Source LLC
Chambersburg PA
CBHW072153160426
43197CB00012B/2368